▶▶▶ **Interpretationshilfen**

Othello

William Shakespeare

W0173592

Cornelsen

Othello · Interpretationshilfen

Erarbeitet von Martina Baasner

Verlagsredaktion
Priscilla Lavodrama

Umschlaggestaltung
Cornelsen Verlag Design / klein & halm Grafikdesign

Umschlagillustration
Shutterstock Creative

Technische Umsetzung
L101 Mediengestaltung, Fürstenwalde

Bildquellen
p. 5: Photoshot. All rights reserved.

www.cornelsen.de

1. Auflage, 1. Druck 2018

© 2018 Cornelsen Verlag GmbH, Berlin

Druck: AZ Druck und Datentechnik GmbH, Kempten

ISBN 978-3-06-036366-7

Contents

All page and line numbers refer to the Cornelsen edition of Othello (ISBN 978-3-06-036363-6) with the exception of cross-references to other sections of this book.

William Shakespeare (1564–1616) ◄◄◄

Surprisingly little is known about William Shakespeare, Britain's national poet and Man of the Millennium, considering that he is probably the most famous playwright who ever lived. He was born in Stratford-upon-Avon in April 1564 and educated in the local grammar school. His father was a glove maker and a member of the town council. At 18, he married Anne Hathaway, with whom he had three children, Susanna, and the twins Hamnet and Judith. Little else is known about

him until 1592, when Shakespeare is mentioned as being a playwright in London. It is also known that he worked as an actor and that he was part owner of a company of actors called 'The Lord Chamberlain's Men', who soon became the leading London theatre company and enjoyed Queen Elizabeth's patronage. After her death in 1603, King James also awarded them a royal patent and the troupe was renamed 'The King's Men'. Shakespeare became a wealthy man and bought properties in London and Stratford. He retired to Stratford in around 1614 and died there on 23 April 1616.

During his lifetime he wrote 38 plays. He may have written more, but these have not survived. Although 18 of his plays were published during his lifetime, most of these editions (called 'quartos') were probably not overseen by Shakespeare. Their texts may have been reconstructed from memory by members of the cast of the plays. It was only in 1623 that his plays were first published by two of his former colleagues in what is called 'The Folio'. But as Shakespeare was by then dead, it cannot be said that the Folio is a definitive text. However, it was the first time that many of his plays, including *Othello*, were printed. Shakespeare is unusual in that he wrote a wide variety of plays. Not only did he write history plays that covered over a hundred years of

English history, he was also equally competent at tragedy (e. g. *Hamlet*) as well as comedy (e. g. *Much Ado about Nothing*). Shakespeare was very good at turning older plays or stories from Greek or Roman mythology into new plays. Besides being a playwright, he was also a prolific poet: he wrote a cycle of 154 sonnets as well as several long poems.

Shakespeare's reputation grew slowly after his death, but by the end of the 20th century, his plays had become the most performed plays in the world. Some theatre companies devoted their repertoire almost exclusively to the performance of his plays, such as Shakespeare's Globe in London or the Royal Shakespeare Company (RSC) in Stratford-upon-Avon. There are annual international festivals in his name and British institutions, such as the BBC and the British Council, produce media to help people understand his language and to facilitate an approach to his dramas. Many of the lines from his plays and poems are still well known today. After his death, his works have inspired adaptations and spin-offs in different art forms throughout the centuries, and they are still considered very relevant today. Shakespeare's characters and their relationships and conflicts have remained timeless, since he never judges human behaviour and experience, but shows them in a touching way audiences or readers can still relate to. He has also coined an astonishing number of new words and managed to evoke gripping moods while giving his characters definitive voices at the same time. His complex or heightened language makes use of many rhetorical figures that make his lines so memorable. It is thought that he has contributed thousands of words to the English language. Shakespeare's inventiveness and creativity laid the groundwork that helped English to become the universal language it is today.

Historical background

Life in Renaissance England

The term 'Renaissance' means 'rebirth' and refers to the revival of interest in Greek and Roman culture, whose influence on Western civilizations had disappeared during the Middle Ages (roughly between 1100–1400). Beginning in Italy in the 14th century, Renaissance ideas spread all over Europe and challenged people's traditional beliefs through inventions and discoveries. Nicolaus Copernicus and Galileo Galilei introduced the idea that the earth revolves around the sun and not the other way around, like claimed in the Bible. Johannes Gutenberg's printing press (invented around 1439) furthered education and the spreading of ideas among the classes formerly restricted to information coming only from the ruling elite and the Church. English explorers, such as Francis Drake or Walter Raleigh, discovered or colonised new worlds through their seafaring missions, bringing back exotic goods and tales of their adventures.

All this opened England to continental and global developments and had an impact on her society and culture, especially on literary movements and playwrights. Shakespeare had a singular gift of using old dramatic or epic forms and combining them with the experiences he had been exposed to.

He would also make use of the concepts governing people's lives, such as the *Chain of Being*, a hierarchical system of divine order that must not be upset. At its top in heaven was God, with the king as his representative on earth and the Head of State, and the Pope as Head of the Church. Below them, arranged in descending order, were placed the nobility, the middle classes, the lower classes, animals, plants and minerals like stones. If this order was disturbed by an unusual event like the killing of the king, the broken chain was equivalent to overall chaos which had to be set right again. In *Othello*, the titular character refers to this state of upheaval when he imagines that his marriage is under threat and he and his wife Desdemona do not love each other anymore (III, iii, ll. 90–92). Another notion of the Elizabethan worldview was that all living beings were made of the four elements: water, earth, fire and air, which had a counterpart in liquid substances in the human body, called *Humours*. A person's temperament depended on the mixture of these humours of blood, melancholy, phlegm and choler. If 'blood' was predominant, one would be cheerful, and respectively melancholic, phlegmatic or choleric. An even balance of the humours meant a good-tempered person. In Othello's case, the element of fire takes over to reign his feelings of rage and, together with his excessive jealousy, makes him an extremely 'ill-humoured' man.

In astronomy, the theory of the old geocentric model with the earth at the centre of the universe had been connected to the *Signs of the Zodiac* as well and was believed to be governing people's natures. Similarly important was the belief that fate, or fortune, was the main controlling force in life, which had the image of *The Wheel of Fortune* as its representation. A person in a high position on top of the wheel could expect to move to a lower place or fall off the wheel altogether. Alternatively, his prospects could improve with a ride from a lower to a higher place. In *Othello*, his officer Iago reproaches the hero with *'Would you would bear your fortune like a man!'* (IV, i, l. 59). At the same time, people believed in man's ability to control his own destiny, but superstition was widespread too, and people also believed in omens and supernatural elements. Whereas other Shakespearean plays deal more extensively with witches and ghosts, there is only a brief reference to magic powers in this tragedy when Othello explains the miraculous qualities of the handkerchief he gave to his wife (III, iv, ll. 53–71), or when a father thinks a daughter was abducted using witchcraft.

Thus, the Elizabethans were in a state of change, and insecurity paired with excitement about developments was common. The different groups in society who had similar aims or religious beliefs tried to assert their interests at a time when political parties didn't yet exist and the monarch had a system of spies to counteract suspected treason. As theatres were a meeting-place for huge crowds, their supervision and control was vital to the authorities. Life expectancy was short, many children did not survive their teenage years nor mothers their childbirth, because illnesses could not be cured. In addition, the plague regularly killed large numbers of people. The English economy relied on agriculture, and the majority of the population were poor labourers and farmers while a rising and socially mobile middle class tried to achieve the wealth and status of the nobility despite the concept of the

Chain of Being. Manufacturing and overseas trade with imports and exports made the merchants prosperous. Shakespeare himself was a wealthy landowner when he retired to his birthplace.

Women were seen as dependent on a male family member or their husbands, and their only occupations were to raise a family and run the household. Despite Queen Elizabeth I's position as a monarch, the women's lot in her country did not improve. Othello's wife, Desdemona, has defied society's moral expectations by eloping and marrying him secretly, but cannot enjoy any other freedom of choice. She argues in front of the Duke of Venice and his senators that her female duty has passed on from father to husband, which is then accepted by her male environment (I, iii, ll. 178–187). Shakespeare puts a number of articulate and intelligent women on stage, who display the equality society denied them, like Emilia in *Othello*. In her speech about married partners, she demands that husbands and wives should have the same rights to act as they wish (IV, iii, ll. 80–99).

At the end of the play, when the villain Iago's confession of his crimes is to be forcefully extracted from him by torture, there is a reference to the cruel punishments of the era (*'Torments will ope[n] your lips.'*, V, ii, l. 303). People utilised brutal public executions for their entertainment, since violence was an integral part of their everyday life.

▶ **Points to remember:**
- Renaissance ideas spread from Italy to England in the 16th century and widened people's horizons in many ways and areas.
- The reawakened interest in Greek and Roman literary works and mythology had a great impact on playwrights.
- People believed in a hierarchical system of order where everyone had his place and chaos would reign if anyone disturbed this structure.
- Elizabethans believed in the concepts of the *Four Humours*, the *Signs of the Zodiac* and the *Wheel of Fortune*.
- All levels of society were spied upon by the monarch's secret agents.
- Life expectancy was short as there were only few cures for illnesses.
- Overseas trade and colonisation brought wealth to the merchants, but the country's economy was based on agriculture and the farmers were poor.

- Women were not independent and had to obey men, they were seen as mothers and housewives only.
- Shakespeare has created two female characters who show some instances of self-confidence in the play.
- Torture and executions were frequent spectacles and crowds watched them for entertainment.

Queen Elizabeth and King James

Queen Elizabeth I, the daughter of Tudor King Henry VIII and his second wife, Anne Boleyn, ruled England for 45 years from 1558 to 1603 in a time of relative prosperity and peace. Her father had cut ties with the Pope and the Catholic Church in order to divorce his first wife, and founded the Anglican (Protestant) Church of which he pronounced himself the Head. Elizabeth's half-sister, Mary, ruled before her and made Catholicism the state religion again. When Elizabeth became queen, she was regarded as an illegitimate child and consequently an illegitimate monarch by many Catholics. She continued her father's religious politics, and Anglicanism has since remained the official state religion. However, religious conflict determined English life throughout her reign, and she was declared a heretic by Rome in 1569, which endangered her throne. Her life was attempted more than once, and some of her aristocrats rebelled against her reign, although the absolute rule of kings was a doctrine Elizabethans believed in. Elizabeth never married and avoided allying with a foreign country or an English political group which might diminish her power. The Spanish fleet sent to overthrow her in 1588 was successfully defeated and led to England's supremacy on the seas.

Elizabeth travelled through her country, inviting herself into the houses of the aristocrats, many of whom she rewarded with important positions at court. The Crown had a reputation for the corruption of the courtiers who wanted to increase their influence. Members of the nobility were intent on living in luxury and acquiring more land as their property. The queen died childless in 1603 and her crown passed to her cousin James VI, King of Scotland, who converted from Catholicism to Anglicanism. His mother, Mary Stuart, Queen of Scots, had been executed for treason against the English throne. Her son became England's King James I and ruled from 1603 to 1625 (Shakespeare died in 1616). His reign was troubled by political and religious controversy, of which the most famous incident was the Gunpowder Plot in 1605, an attempt to assassinate the king.

▶ **Points to remember:**
- Queen Elizabeth I continued her father Henry VIII's religious politics and kept England Protestant.
- She faced opposition from the Pope and Catholics in her country and abroad in regard to the legitimacy of her rulership.
- Despite rebellions and attempts on her life, the queen ruled for 45 years and she never married.
- Her courtiers lived a life in luxury and corruption at court was commonplace.
- After Queen Elizabeth's death in 1603, the son of the Scottish queen became England's new King James I.

Muslims and Black Africans

Othello is called 'The Moor of Venice' in the subtitle of the play, which suggests a dark-skinned man for modern readers, but Elizabethans used the term to describe lighter-skinned North Africans or generally Muslims as well. The painting of the Moorish Ambassador (SB p. 12) from Barbary (the Berber coastal regions of North Africa) shows a diplomat from a Muslim state who visited Queen Elizabeth I's court in order to propose an alliance with England in the fight against Spain. North African Muslims were then regarded as political allies against England's enemies, but were also approached with hostility and fear. Especially Turkish Muslims (called the 'Ottomites' in the play) were seen as a potential danger for the whole of Europe, too, because the expansion of the Ottoman Empire had led them as far as Vienna. Reports of the Turks' cruelty towards the people whose country they invaded made them fearsome enemies. Claiming his loyalty to Venice at the end of the play, Othello himself boasts about killing a *'turbaned Turk'*, *'a circumcisèd dog'* who had spoken ill of Venice and beaten a Venetian (V, ii, ll. 348–352).

Shakespeare must have met Black Africans, too, who sometimes were high-status visitors on diplomatic missions, artists or members of merchants' crews, but the majority of blacks were either free men and women or slaves working in different trades. They were also part of the royal court and the houses of the Queen's noblemen. In 1601, a proclamation stated that 'too many Negras' from England's archeneemy Spain had come to the country, and, not being Protestant Christians, should be expelled. In an account of his life, Othello speaks about being of royal African parentage and that he was sold into slavery and later rescued (I, iii, l. 137). He must have been baptised, because he refers to his Christian values and reproaches his drunk and unruly officers with behaving unmannerly like *'Turks'* (II, iii, ll. 152–154). The stereotypical view in those days, however, was that people with black skin were thought of as being inferior and basically of beastly nature in comparison to those of white skin. Shakespeare decided not to reflect the prejudice in his portrayal of Othello at the beginning of the play, but shows him as having prestige and being highly praised for his military skills as an army general. The city-state of Venice with its cosmopolitan population was tolerant of foreigners and awarded its mercenary soldiers with high positions. The Duke of Venice holds Othello in high esteem and entrusts him with an important military mission in Cyprus, a Venetian colony that is under threat of a Turkish invasion. Senator Brabantio, in whose house Othello is a frequent guest, also fully trusts Othello and enjoys listening to his tales of warfare and adventures, and for this, his daughter Desdemona admires and loves him deeply. In the first scene of act I, several Venetian characters openly use racial epithets to describe Othello and his alleged deeds (Roderigo: *'thick lips'*, l. 67; *'lascivious Moor'*, l. 125; Iago: *'old black ram'*, l. 89; *'Barbary horse'*, l. 112). Even though Othello's status is high, his adversaries define him via his skin colour and are not willing to see him as equal or as a potential son-in-law. In Cyprus, there is no open or veiled discrimination, and Iago, Othello's flag-bearer and the villain of the play, refrains from making racist remarks, but describes his superior in a fair manner. Later in the play, however, Shakespeare's portrait of the jealous Othello as a violent and murderous savage seems to reinforce the stereotype of the 'barbarous Moor'. Without Iago's malevolent and treacherous scheming, Othello would not have turned into a raving lunatic. On the other hand, Shakespeare might just have used the character as he was presented in his source story and might have wanted to explore the tragic flaw of excessive jealous rage. Possibly the playwright also wanted to examine racism but did not intend to make it the focus of the tragedy, or the exploration would have taken up more room. In our time, racism is a topic discussed in view of political correctness, which was an unfamiliar concept for Shakespeare's contemporaries.

Though today Othello is usually played by a black actor, it cannot be safely said whether Shakespeare had a North African or a sub-Saharan African in mind for this role. Roderigo's racist slur (*'thick-lips'*, I, 1, l. 67) may point to a man with a darker colour.

▶ **Points to remember:**
- For Elizabethans, the term 'Moor' could refer to a man from North Africa, from the sub-Saharan region or generally to a Muslim.
- Muslims from North Africa were welcome as political allies against England's enemy, Catholic Spain, but were regarded with hostility.
- Turkish Muslims were feared because of their aggressive invasions and violence against people in Europe.
- Black Africans in England were diplomats, artists, members of aristocratic households, tradesmen, free men or women and slaves.
- In 1601, the Crown declared that there were too many blacks who should leave the country.
- People viewed dark-skinned foreigners in a stereotypical way, namely as inferior, animal-like and lustful.
- Shakespeare draws a completely different portrait of Othello, showing him as a noble, efficient and highly esteemed individual who only changes into a man committing barbarous acts when he gets deceived and plagued by the villain Iago.
- The topic 'racism' as we know it today did not exist in Shakespeare's time.

Venice and Cyprus

For Elizabethans, setting a play in Venice bore particular associations. This unique city-republic was ruled by an aristocrat chosen by his peers, who did not hold a hereditary position like that of the English king. The Duke of Venice or 'Doge' was the highest judge and foreigners doing trade in Venice or working in important professions were guaranteed equality before the law and the freedom to all rights and privileges of the Venetians. Cosmopolitan Venice had an ethnically mixed population and a reputation for tolerance.

England's merchants must have viewed it as a paradise due to the important global trade in commercial goods that took place on the Rialto Bridge. The well-being of the city relied on its role as a centre of European business and finance.

On the other hand, Venice was famous for never-ending festivities, loose manners and sexual liberty. Its women were generally seen as courtesans or prostitutes who lived their lives in sin. As the actual prostitutes were often elegant and cultured women, dressing like upper-class ladies, it is easy for Iago to pretend that Othello's Venetian wife might be a courtesan or open to other men's advances, too.

Cyprus is important in that it is so different from Venice and, as its colony overseen by a governor, a place without the strict Venetian social rules. In Cyprus, Shakespeare shows his characters as less reserved and mannerly than in Venice and more prone to immoderate behaviour.

▶ **Points to remember:**
- Venice was a city-state with a ruler chosen by the nobility, who was also the highest judge.
- It was Europe's business and financial centre with important global trade.
- Venice's population was ethnically mixed and foreigners had the same rights as Venetians.
- Venetian women were reputed to have loose manners and be ready for sexual adventures.
- Cyprus was a Venetian colony supervised by a governor.

The Theatre

The first commercial theatre in England simply called 'The Theatre' was built in 1576 by James Burbage, who would later become Shakespeare's associate. The London Common Council forbade theatres within the city walls, and people commonly regarded actors and playwrights as low-life characters, little better than criminals. Next to the theatre buildings outside the city other entertainments, such as taverns, brothels, cockfighting or bear-baiting arenas, were situated. Burbage built his theatre on the shore of the Thames River, in Shoreditch. However, Shakespeare and his actors managed to secure the patronage of a nobleman and later even that of the monarch. They became popular entertainment at Queen Elizabeth's and King James' court. Their financial success gave Shakespeare and his shareholders the funds to build the Globe playhouse in 1599. There, James Burbage's son Richard, Will Kempe, Edward Alleyn and other players performed in the plays Shakespeare wrote for them for many years and established their excellent reputation.

Shakespeare may have found his love for the theatre by watching travelling acting companies who came to the countryside where he lived. The troupes would transport their property on wagons and use inns or courtyards to perform their plays, because there had not been any buildings for theatres. They mostly showed religious stories or scenes taken from the Bible, which meant to teach viewers a lesson in morals. Two characters in *Othello*, Desdemona and Iago, can be seen as stereotypical characters embodying good and evil in humankind and serve as an example of how (not) to behave as proper Christians. During the Renaissance, the plays would become less religious and would be based on Greek or Roman legends or have historical events as their plot.

The Master of the Revels, a public official, had to read and approve every play to be performed and was authorised to shut down theatres completely. During times of plague or social or political riots, authorities would close the theatres, which they feared were places of moral corruption. Audiences were packed with people from all walks of life – it is said that a full house at the Globe numbered about 3.000 spectators. The rich patrons sat on the stage or on gallery seats, whereas the poorer visitors called 'groundlings' stood in front of the stage that was about a metre above the ground. These 'groundlings' paid a penny for the entertainment, which was a day's wage. Audience behaviour was quite different then, with people eating, drinking and smoking during the performance and heckling players or even throwing things at them. Shakespeare wrote for his diverse audience and suited his language and the characters, actions and situations to all levels of his society.

The theatre buildings were round and roofless with a thrust stage (projecting out into the audience), and plays were staged during the day. A performance could take half a day – today Shakespeare's plays are usually cut because they can last up to four hours. The sets were bare and props would be carried on by the players. If a bed had to be put on stage like in the last scene of *Othello*, it would be done in full view of the audience, because there were no breaks or intervals. If a scene was set at night, the actors would comment on the moon or stars in the sky to indicate the hour of the day. The actors did not wear the costumes indicated for the time the plays were set in, but their normal clothes. However, they had elegant hand-me-down clothes from the upper classes for royalty shown on stage.

Most plays were rehearsed for just a day or two, they ran only for a short time and players had to learn their parts for a new play quickly. Full scripts did not exist, but the actors only had their own lines on paper slips with the cues of the previous speaker so that they knew when to say their lines. Some theatres staged up to four different plays within a week. Female roles were performed by boys and young men, because women were not permitted to act on stage until 1660. As Shakespeare often used the motif of cross-dressing, when female characters (played by boys) dressed as boys on stage, this allowed much room for double meaning.

The Globe burned down in 1613 when the roof caught fire after a cannon had been fired during a performance. In the 1990s, a reconstruction of the old Globe was built very close to its original site, where, today, visitors can experience plays the way Elizabethans did.

In 1642, the Puritans, a very strict religious faction that saw performing and watching plays as immoral, succeeded in closing the theatres altogether. They did not reopen until Charles II came to the throne 18 years later. By then, many of the theatrical traditions of

Shakespeare's theatre were lost, and the new theatres of the Restoration period viewed and staged his plays very differently.

To get an idea of what the Globe building looked like, take the virtual tour offered in this free mobile app: *Shakespeare's Globe 360*

▶ **Points to remember:**
- Theatres were not allowed within the London city walls because actors were thought of as vagabonds.
- Shakespeare must have seen travelling players in Stratford who performed simple stories, e.g. from the Bible.
- In London, his troupe secured royal patronage.
- Their company built the Globe playhouse in 1599, which burnt down in 1613.
- Shakespeare wrote his plays for a very diverse audience and adjusted language and action to serve everyone.
- During riots or outbreaks of the plague, the theatres would be closed since they held so many people.
- A censor, called the Master of the Revels, had to approve each play.
- Performances took place during the day, and time and place of the scenes were indicated by the dialogue; scene changes did not exist.
- Actors only had their parts on a slip of paper, there were no full scripts.
- Rehearsal time was just a few days, and some theatres put on up to four plays a week.
- Women were not allowed on stage, and their roles were played by boys and young men.
- In 1642, the Puritans, a strict religious sect, were successful in shutting down all theatres which reopened only in 1660.
- Close to the original site, a reconstruction of the old Globe was built in the 1990s.

English Renaissance Drama

In medieval times, plays took the form of folk tales or stories from the Christian tradition which were meant to strengthen people's belief in religion and to teach them moral behaviour. In the 'Mystery Plays', dramatic Bible scenes were reenacted. 'Morality Plays' with their stock situation of the fight between good and evil (or 'Virtue' and 'Vice'), in which the good character invariably wins after having been severely tempted by the devilish character, were very popular for hundreds of years. The other characters were allegories or personifications of positive and negative human qualities, such as Strength, Charity, Mercy, Greed, Lust and Envy, which were shown in a dilemma the viewers could relate to. Gradually, plays would feature more secular content and show characters with more personal struggles in the so-called 'Interludes' of the 16th century. The reawakened interest in ancient Greek and Roman literary forms had its influence too, and comedies, tragedies and classical texts by Plautus, Seneca, Plutarch and Ovid were inspiration and models for dramatists.

Shakespeare's plots were inspired by other Renaissance playwrights preceding his career, such as Thomas Kyd (1558–1594) or Christopher Marlowe (1564–1593), who had written very popular plays. Kyd's *Spanish Tragedy*, a very bloody tale of vengeance, contained elements like extremes of emotion, deception, revenge and justice, which can also be found in *Othello*. Marlowe's dramatic works *Tamburlaine the Great*, *The Jew of Malta* and *Dr Faustus* threw a spotlight on strong characters who had complex personalities and experienced conflicting emotions, like all of Shakespeare's tragic heroes.

▶ **Points to remember:**
- In the Middle Ages, 'Mystery Plays' (Biblical scenes) and 'Morality Plays' (allegorical characters struggling with temptation) were popular for a long time.
- More secular plays called 'Interludes' showing individual characters replaced the religious plays in the 16th century.
- Elizabethan playwrights looked at Greek and Roman plays and literary texts for inspiration.
- Thomas Kyd and Christopher Marlowe were successful dramatists and made characters display extreme emotions on stage.

Tragedy

The literary genre of tragedy has its origin in ancient Greece and depicts human suffering brought about unavoidably by a character's own actions and ends in the hero's death and catastrophe. Aristotle (384-322 BC), the Greek philosopher, defined tragedy as a play in which the main character, a person of high status, is afflicted by trouble caused by the gods, a flaw of character or a mistake in judgement whereby his surroundings are deeply affected as well. As a rule, the plot shows the stages of the protagonist's fall, who finally recognises what causes his suffering before he dies. The intended effect on the viewers is to arouse pity and fear, which is meant to purify their thoughts and emotions (catharsis).

During King James' reign the specific genre of 'revenge tragedy' was very popular. In it, the characters seek vengeance for a wrong committed, either against honour or God's commandments. These plays tended to be very bloodthirsty and enacted violence and murder on stage. A typical stereotype of this genre is the 'malcontent', an individual who is critical of others or of society in general, and frequently plots against them. Since England had turned to Protestantism, strong anti-Catholicism prevailed and found its way into the plays. The popular prejudice was that in Catholic countries like Italy or Spain, where many of these plays were set, intrigue, corruption and sexual passion were commonplace.

Othello is considered to be one of Shakespeare's supreme tragedies next to *Hamlet*, *Macbeth* and *King Lear*, which were all written in the same decade. It is believed to have been written between 1600–1605. The play does not have politics or the fall of princes or kings as its focus, but Othello's personal psychological situation. After Othello's death, the Venetian state will not collapse, however, the characters in his personal environment involved in the villain Iago's machinations must die undeservedly. The play is therefore also called a 'domestic' tragedy. Unlike the Italian characters, Iago, Roderigo and Brabantio, who frankly voice their contemptuous views of foreigners, the Duke of Venice's court does not reflect intolerance or corruption, and he himself is shown as competent, understanding and fair. Although *Othello* is not a proper revenge tragedy, one of its features is embodied by Iago

– he is the malcontent schemer planning to take revenge for the humiliation he has suffered.

Following classical dramatic theory, Elizabethan playwrights divided a drama into five distinctive sections. The action begins with the exposition, which introduces the main characters and the plot and is then driven forward by the inciting moment, i.e. an event which leads to a conflict or problem that needs to be solved during the play. Further conflicts complicate the plot, and the characters meet more obstacles in the next phase, the rising action. Often, there are sub-plots mirroring the theme or action of the main plot, which are usually resolved before the ending of the main action. The highest point of tension is reached with the climax or turning-point, which marks a complete change for the hero for the better (in a comedy) or the worse (in a tragedy). The following part is called the falling action, which is usually shorter than the rising action, and contains developments leading to the resolution (in a comedy) or the catastrophe (in a tragedy) that end the play. In comedies, the characters are reconciled and marriages are likely, whereas the hero of a tragedy dies.

▶ **Points to remember:**
- A tragedy deals with a character who brings unavoidable suffering on himself by his deeds and dies at the end.
- Aristotle defines a tragic hero as one who has a flaw of character or misjudges a situation completely.
- The action is supposed to raise pity and fear among the viewers, which purifies their thoughts and emotions (catharsis).
- Revenge tragedies, often extremely bloodthirsty plays, were very popular.
- The character of the 'malcontent' was a common stereotype who was critical of others and plotting against them.
- Anti-Catholic attitudes found their way into plays.
- *Othello* is one of the four most famous Shakespearean tragedies and was written between 1600–1605.
- It is a 'domestic tragedy' dealing with Othello's personal situation, not with politics or the succession of a kingdom.
- Iago embodies the 'malcontent' figure, though *Othello* is not a typical revenge tragedy.

- Plays had a five-act structure with an exposition, an inciting moment that sets the action in motion, rising action up to the climax, falling action and finally the resolution (comedies) or catastrophe (tragedies).

Shakespeare's Source

Shakespeare's main source for *Othello* was the story 'Un capitano moro' from the collection *Gli Hecatommithi* (= The Hundred Tales) by Giovanni Battista Giraldi, aka Cinthio (1565/6), which he transformed into dramatic form.

▶▶▶ The Story

The story of *Othello* is quickly told, because the play has a simple plot: Othello is a black army general in the service of Venice, who is persuaded by his resentful flag-bearer Iago that his wife Desdemona is unfaithful. Driven to extreme jealous rage, Othello murders her and only then finds out about Iago's deception and her innocence upon which he kills himself.

There is no sub-plot, which Shakespeare often made use of in other plays. The first act is set in Venice and could be seen as a prologue to what happens in the rest of the drama set in Cyprus to where the characters are sent in a military context. On their journey, a storm hits the travellers' ships, which predicts the emotional chaos that follows. The action in Cyprus takes place in a condensed period of some thirty-six hours, which almost corresponds to the Aristotelian concept of unity of action, place and time.

Act I

Scene 1: The play opens with a dramatic entrance in a dark street in Venice at night. Two men, the soldier Iago and the gentleman Roderigo, are in the middle of a discussion, in which Iago complains of having been passed over for promotion by his superior officer, who is not named. We learn later that it is Othello, a black army general in the service of the Venetian state. Instead of Iago, Cassio was promoted, who is a military theorist, but has little practical experience in leading soldiers. There is a range of swearwords, and the tone is angry in this heated argument (*'Tush! never tell me […].'*, l. 1; *'Sblood, but you will not hear me […].'*, l. 4). This raises suspense, because the audience will want to find out what the quarrel is about and what the money was used for. Roderigo complains that Iago has used his money but did not inform him about important matters that are not immediately disclosed to the viewers. Iago denies this and explains in detail what his motives and plans are. He hates Othello and wants to take revenge for the slight he suffered. He finds a willing accomplice in Roderigo, who bears his own grudge against Othello. Iago makes it clear from the start that he will pretend to be a loyal officer to Othello but will in fact follow his own agenda ('*I am not what I am*', l. 66). He suggests to Roderigo that the two wake up the respected Senator Brabantio and inform him that his daughter Desdemona has run away with Othello. Shouting from the street, they do so, using racial slurs against Othello and describing obscenities (Roderigo: '*thick-lips*', l. 67; '*lascivious Moor*', l. 125; Iago: '*an old black ram is tupping your white ewe*', ll. 89–90; '*Barbary horse*', l. 112; '*your daughter and the Moor are now making the beast with two backs*', ll. 115–116). Iago leaves the scene before Brabantio can find out that he has been involved and tells Roderigo that the runaway couple can be found at the Sagittary Inn. After Brabantio has searched the house for Desdemona in vain and come downstairs, he expresses his extreme upset about his daughter's disobedience and flight, which he can only explain with the use of potions or magic (in those days a serious offence with deadly consequences for the accused). Roderigo is found to be an unwelcome suitor interested in Desdemona himself, but now Brabantio is content to have him at his side when putting together a search party to find the missing Desdemona.

The way Othello and Desdemona are talked about by other characters is not very flattering. He is reproached with using unnatural means to steal a rich white woman from her father's house, and she has flouted the expectations of female duty and honour, which brings great shame onto her father's head. It is Iago who is the driving force in making this public and his further plans are only known to himself and Roderigo.

What impressions does Shakespeare convey of the Venetian society and the characters present in this scene?
Why does Shakespeare inform the audience from the start that Iago will deceive Othello?

Scene 2: Brabantio has drummed up his men and other citizens in search of Desdemona and Othello. On a dark byroad in front of the Sagittary Inn, Othello is warned by Iago that Brabantio and his party are on their way to have him arrested, i.e. for drawing Desdemona to '*[his] sooty bosom*' (l. 70) by unlawful means. Brabantio seems to be seriously insulted by his daughter's marriage to a man of African descent, which he categorically disagrees with on racial grounds. Iago also tells Othello the lie that he wanted to stab Roderigo for insulting Othello and advises him to go inside, which Othello refuses. Othello remains calm and dignified, being convinced that the duke will not take action against an officer who has served the Venetian state so well. Cassio, Othello's second-in-command and newly appointed lieutenant, arrives with a search party from the duke who urgently demands to see Othello for an important military mission. Before they can leave, Brabantio and Roderigo appear with an armed party and accuse Othello of seducing and abducting Desdemona. Brabantio offends Othello with strong words (*'foul thief'*, l. 62; *'damned as thou art'*, l. 63; *'such a thing as thou'*, l. 71) when asking where Desdemona is, who, in his opinion, would never have married a man like Othello. Earlier, she has spurned *'the wealthy curlèd darlings of our nation'* (l. 68), i.e. the eligible young Venetian aristocrats who wanted to marry her. He orders his men to arrest Othello and insists that the case should be brought before the duke. Othello remains unfazed, asks everyone to calm down and informs Brabantio that the duke has sent for him on state business. Brabantio agrees to postpone the matter for the moment and present his case at the ducal court, the highest court of justice and authority in Venice.

In what way does the audience's view of Othello change after seeing him in person?

Scene 3: The duke and his senators are in session discussing urgent political matters in the council chamber of the duke's palace, particularly the threatening manoeuvres of 230 Turkish warships apparently sailing towards Cyprus, then a Venetian colony. They see through a ploy which is intended to make them think the Turks will attack Rhodes. When Othello, Brabantio, Iago, Roderigo and others arrive at the court, Brabantio accuses Othello of seducing and abducting his daughter. Although the duke has other matters of the highest concern on his mind than dealing with matters of private importance, his senator Brabantio gets a hearing, because he is so upset. In front of the senators, Othello does not rise to any insult, a man with a clear conscience, in full knowledge of his merits in the service of the State of Venice. Radi-

ating authority, he tells the senators plainly and truthfully what led to
his marriage with Desdemona. Othello recounts that he was a frequent
guest in Brabantio's household, where his daughter avidly listened to
the story of his life. His adventures as well as tales of his battles fasci-
nated her. She loves him for the dangers he has passed, and he loves
her for the pity she feels for him. Equally impressed by Othello's account, the duke can understand the admiration a woman might feel for
a man with such unusual experiences. Othello suggests summoning
Desdemona to verify his account and sends Iago to fetch her from the
Sagittary Inn. She confirms everything Othello has said and tells her
father that she still respects him, but that her loving duty as a wife be-
longs to her husband now ('*I do perceive here a divided duty.*', l. 179). The
duke tries to console Brabantio, who glumly accepts his daughter's decision and lays off further proceedings ('*If virtue no delighted duty lack,
your son-in-law is far more fair than black.*', ll. 285–286). In the mean-
time, military threats have accumulated. Othello is posted to Cyprus
the same night to deal with the imminent threat of an invasion by the
Turks in Cyprus and lead the defence as the new governor. Desdemona begs the duke to let her accompany her husband, which he grants,
but Othello won't allow her on board his front-line battleship. Out of
loving care he entrusts her to Iago on board a supply vessel in the rear,
with Iago's wife Emilia to attend her. Brabantio leaves and warns Othello that Desdemona might deceive him, too, like she did with her father. Meanwhile, Roderigo, who is suffering from unrequited love for
Desdemona, is pacified somewhat by Iago who tells him that young
Desdemona's love for a man so far advanced in years cannot last long.
Iago feels scorn for Roderigo's lovesick complaints and urges him to
help him get revenge, because this will also benefit Roderigo's concern. For this, he needs money, which Roderigo is ready to provide.
Since Othello's marriage has been condoned by Brabantio and the
duke, Iago changes his plans of revenge and aims to make Othello jealous of Cassio and thus ruin both men's lives, which he lets the audience know when he is alone on stage. Saying that Othello is of a '*free
and open nature*' (l. 379) whom he can make believe what he tells him,
Iago is shown as not really racist but only so when he thinks it useful.
He also notes that there are rumours that Emilia has slept with

Othello, which he will accept as the truth, although he seems somewhat indifferent to it.

To what extent have your impressions of Othello and Desdemona and their relationship changed?
Both the Duke of Venice and Brabantio only appear in this act. What do you think is their function in the play?
What is your view of Iago's attitude and schemes?

Act II

Scene1: Montano, Governor of Cyprus, and some other gentlemen are on the lookout for the Turkish fleet that threatens the island of Cyprus when a messenger enters to tell them that the hostile fleet has been scattered and smashed to bits and pieces in a fierce storm. One by one, the Venetian ships arrive safely with Cassio coming in first, who confirms the news of the shipwrecks but worries that Othello's ship might have been lost in the storm. He is followed by Iago's ship with his wife Emilia, Desdemona and Roderigo on board. Everyone is relieved and happy when Othello's ship is spotted. Waiting for Othello to arrive, Desdemona and Iago joke about the nature of women with Iago portraying them generally as false and sex-starved. Desdemona exchanges witticisms with Iago but does not take him too seriously. Cassio takes her hand and speaks to her privately, which Iago wrongly describes as flirtatious behaviour, for it fits in nicely with his devious scheming. Allowing himself to kiss Emilia, Cassio calls this only courtesy while Iago resents Emilia for it, making disparaging remarks. When Othello and his attendants finally arrive, he is welcomed lovingly by his wife Desdemona. He professes his great love for her: *'If I were now to die, 'twere now to be most happy [...].'* (ll. 182–183). They all soon make their way to the castle leaving Roderigo and Iago on their own. Iago tells Roderigo that Desdemona is obviously already in love with Cassio, which could be seen in their intimate moment together. Roderigo thinks it was just courtesy, but Iago convinces him otherwise. Totally in love with Desdemona, Roderigo listens to every word Iago says, who suggests Roderigo to pick up a quarrel with Cassio and thereby get him out of the way. Roderigo agrees and leaves. Alone, Iago reveals his secret thoughts again: he thinks it likely that Cassio loves Desdemona and he himself would like to sleep with her out of revenge for Emilia's suspected infidelity. At any rate, the confrontation between Roderigo and Cassio will serve to make Othello jealous and drive him mad.

How do you assess Roderigo and Cassio's character and behaviour up to this point?
Describe the way in which the women in this society are treated and how they react to it.

Scene 2: A herald announces that since the Turkish threat has been lifted, General Othello has ordered festivities for all to celebrate his wedding and the destruction of the Turkish fleet. Everyone should be jubilant at the prospect of enjoying Cyprian wine and food aplenty.

Scene 3: Before retiring with Desdemona for their wedding night – due to the adverse circumstances the marriage has not yet been con- summated – Othello orders Cassio and Iago to stand watch for the night and see to it that the men on guard behave properly. Iago insinu- ates that Desdemona might be interested in other men, but Cassio does not believe this. Having been told by Cassio that he has no toler- ance for alcohol, Iago cunningly invites Cassio to a cup of wine, fully aware that it will not do Cassio any good. When the former governor, Montano, and others join them, Cassio cannot refuse to toast Othel- lo's health repeatedly. Iago behaves sociably and sings two songs to encourage more drinking. He talks about the drinking habits of differ- ent nations and believes the English superior in holding their drink. Completely drunk, but insisting he is sober, Cassio staggers back to his watch. During his absence, Iago speaks with Montano about Cassio's alleged drinking problem, worrying that he might not be able to deal with his professional responsibilities. When Montano advises him to tell Othello about this, Iago pretends that he will try to help Cassio first. When Roderigo comes in, Iago sends him off to get rid of Cassio. But the tables are turned quickly. Cassio returns, having Roderigo at his sword point. Montano gets in between them to prevent further fighting but is accidentally gravely wounded by Cassio. The turmoil gets worse, and Iago sends Roderigo to raise an alarm. Othello appears with some attendants and puts an end to the fight. Being only vaguely told by the men what has happened and extremely angered, Othello orders Iago to tell the truth about the conflict, who gives an edited report. Iago supposedly finds it painful to blame Cassio but follows Othello's orders. He says that while he and Montano were talking, Cassio chased a man inside with a drawn sword (Roderigo is not named). Montano stepped between them, while Iago went outside after the unknown man, but could not catch him (which is a lie). Montano and Cassio were fighting when Iago returned. He tries to excuse Cassio's actions by saying that the unknown man must have offended him. In his report, Iago deliberately omits that he made Roderigo do all this and sent him to raise an alarm to make the matter public. His false report underlines his duplicity for the audience and serves to assure Othello and Cassio of Iago's 'honesty'. Othello demotes Cassio for disorderly behaviour. Meanwhile, Desdemona has arrived because of the noise and is led back to bed by Othello, who also sees to Montano's wounds. Cassio is devastated and does not remember much of the events. He regrets his actions deeply, lamenting the loss of his post and reputation (*'I have lost the immortal part of myself, and what remains is bestial.'*, ll. 244–245). Iago proposes that Cassio could seek Desdemona's help in pleading with Othello for the young and handsome officer's reinstatement, which Cassio agrees to. In a third monologue, Iago muses that such an attempt could indicate to Othello that his wife is only pleading in Cassio's favour because she is sexually interested in him. When Roderigo enters and complains that he is now penniless, was beaten and has not enjoyed Desdemona's favours yet, Iago tells him to be patient and appreciate the fact that their first aim of getting Cassio dismissed has been achieved. Alone again, Iago outlines his plan to engineer a meeting between Cassio and Desdemona and sees to it that Othello observes this.

Being told all about Iago's schemes, what will the audience's feelings and reactions be when they watch the action unfold?

Act III

Scene 1: It is important for Cassio to speak to Desdemona, as he feels she is the only one able and willing to plead with Othello for Cassio's reinstatement as lieutenant. Trying to regain his favour, he asks a group of musicians he has hired earlier to play beneath Othello's and Desdemona's window, but a servant (the clown) comes down and sends the musicians away. Cassio gives the man a gold piece and asks him to fetch Emilia. When Iago enters, Cassio tells him about the servant's errand, and Iago promises to send Emilia himself. He also proposes to get Othello out of the way so Cassio can talk to Othello's wife alone. When Emilia arrives, she tells Cassio that Othello and Desdemona have talked about his dismissal, but that, due to Montano's high standing in Cyprus, Othello cannot reinstate him after his obvious public misbehaviour. However, he will try to do so at the earliest opportunity. Cassio then begs Emilia to arrange a meeting with Desdemona, which she is willing to do. All this, of course, suits scheming Iago very well.

Point out the differences between Othello's and Desdemona's relationship and that of Iago and his wife.

Scene 2: Othello decides to inspect the fortifications, taking some Cypriot gentlemen along. Before doing so, he hands over some important letters to Iago to be dispatched by ship to the senate in Venice.

The extreme shortness of this scene (like II, 2) has prompted some directors to cut it altogether. Find reasons why Shakespeare saw fit to place the scene here.

Scene 3: Cassio is relieved and grateful when Desdemona, assisted by Emilia, earnestly pledges to support him to regain his position ('*For thy solicitor shall rather die than give thy cause away.*', ll. 27–28). Feeling unable to meet Othello, he leaves in a hurry when he sees Othello and Iago approaching from a distance. Iago uses this fact to cast some doubt on Cassio's integrity. Desdemona quite frankly tells her husband that Cassio has come to see her asking for help in matters of his reinstatement. She reminds Othello of Cassio's role during their courtship and begs him to reconsider his decision. Othello is not adverse to Cassio's reinstatement but points out that he had to punish him due to public resentment. Although he says '*I will deny thee nothing*' twice (ll. 76; 83), he refuses three times to see Cassio at the times proposed by Desdemona and asks her to leave.

When the two men are alone, Iago asks leading questions and drops false hints about Cassio's intentions, at the same time declaring him an honest man. He warns Othello to maintain his good name and male honour ('*Who steals my purse steals is trash […] but he that filches from me my good name robs me of that which not enriches him, and makes me poor indeed.*', ll. 158–162). He tells Othello to look after his wife and to observe her well when she is with Cassio, reminding him that she readily deceived her father and might betray her husband, too. Thus he plants the idea of Desdemona having an affair with Cassio in Othello's mind, warning him of jealousy, '*the green-eyed monster*' (l. 167), at the same time. Othello denies that he is jealous but begins to believe in Iago's perfidious lies. In ll. 202–205, Iago refers to the behaviour of Venetian wives, saying that wives commit acts of adultery or wicked sexual acts with their lovers, which they would not do with their husbands. He even goes as far as implying that choosing a man like Othello shows how 'unnatural' Desdemona is (ll. 229–234). Growing increasingly doubtful of his wife's virtue and faithfulness, Othello tells Iago to have Emilia watch over her when Cassio is present, who then leaves to do so. Iago's malicious machinations gather speed and begin to bear fruit. More and more uneasy about his own worth and merits and unhappy about his wife's supposed infidelity, Othello suffers from a bout of suspicion and jealousy, which is expressed in a soliloquy. He even curses marriage (ll. 274–278) and thinks being a cuckold (the husband of an unfaithful wife) is the '*plague of great ones*' (l. 274), never distrusting Iago for a second, who has been his flag-bearer for a long time ('*This fellow's of exceeding honesty […].*', l. 259).

When Desdemona summons Othello to dinner, he hides his agitation and pretends to suffer from a headache which Desdemona tries to soothe away using her handkerchief. When he puts it away because it is too small, she drops it. They leave to go to dinner, and Emilia picks the handkerchief up and shows it to Iago, who has wanted it for some reason he did not tell Emilia about. He snatches it away from her and refuses to disclose what he will do with it. Alone on stage, he says he intends to put it in Cassio's lodgings for him to find it.

When Othello returns, he is disillusioned with his life as a soldier and says he would have preferred to live on unwittingly. He demands *'ocular proof'* (l. 361), i.e. hard evidence of Desdemona's disloyalty. Telling him that catching her sleeping with Cassio might be difficult to bring about, Iago offers Othello circumstantial evidence. Firstly, he claims that, while sleeping in a room with Cassio, he watched him behaving and speaking fondly about Desdemona in his sleep as if he were intimate with her. These graphic images enrage Othello so much that he says he will *'tear her all to pieces'* (l. 432). Iago, lying barefacedly, warns Othello of being too rash in his conclusions, as the words were spoken in a dream. Secondly, he then asks him if Othello has seen the handkerchief with the strawberry pattern lately and informs him that Cassio was wiping his beard with it, although it must be in Iago's own pocket at this moment. In a fit of passion, plagued by jealousy and hatred, and believing every word Iago has said, Othello orders Iago to kill Cassio. Instead of first talking to his wife in an attempt to find out what happened, Othello sinks deeply into the self-inflicted pit of misery and self-destruction. He kneels down and vows to avenge himself on Cassio and Desdemona. Having reached his aim, Iago vows to murder Cassio within three days and says *'I am your own forever.'* (l. 480). Othello promotes Iago to lieutenant and will devise a way to kill his wife.

In the course of this so-called 'Temptation Scene', Othello undergoes a complete change of opinion and experiences a wide range of feelings when talking to Iago. Point out key moments of these developments and say who is in control at what moment.
Explain the tactics Iago uses and why he is so successful at his deception.

Scene 4: Desdemona sends the servant to ask Cassio to come and speak with her. She wonders where her handkerchief is, but Emilia does not tell her what she did with it. When Othello comes in asking for the handkerchief, Desdemona denies having lost it but says she cannot produce it at this instant. He tells her about its special powers and value and warns her not ever to lose it. Believing that he only wants to distract her from pleading for Cassio, Desdemona continues speaking on his behalf, which contributes so much to Othello's rage that he leaves in a fury. When Cassio arrives with Iago, Desdemona tells him that her pleading has not gone well for the moment, since Othello seems to be too impatient to be able to listen to anything. Iago leaves to speak to Othello about this matter.

Emilia thinks Othello is just jealous, while Desdemona believes him to be upset by pending matters of state. She thinks he cannot be jealous, because she did not give him any reason to be, whereas Emilia knows that jealousy needs no reason and engenders its own suspicion. Both leave to look for Othello, asking Cassio to wait for a while. Bianca, Cassio's lover, enters and complains of having been neglected by him. He, though, does not seem to care much, asking her to copy the embroidery of Desdemona's handkerchief instead. Bianca suspects that it is a gift from another woman, but Cassio tells her truthfully that he found it in his room. He sends her away, saying that he needs to see Othello, which Bianca grudgingly accepts.

Examine the role and function of the handkerchief in scenes 3 and 4 of this act.

Act IV

Scene 1: Iago torments Othello even further with malicious insinuations and vivid descriptions of Desdemona's and Cassio's lovemaking, maintaining that Desdemona has an affair with the latter whom she has allegedly given the precious handkerchief and who supposedly boasts of having slept with her (*'Her honour is an essence that's not seen; they have it very oft that have it not.'*, ll. 16–17). Overcome by jealousy and rage, Othello falls into an epileptic fit. Cassio enters while Othello is unconscious and wants to look after him, but Iago says Othello will recover on his own. Iago's calm reaction and matter-of-fact way to deal with Othello's seizure shows that this is a common occurrence (*'he had one yesterday'*, l. 49). The two men continue talking while Othello is lying on stage and Iago uses the instant to orchestrate his next step, asking Cassio to return later when Othello is better. After Cassio's exit,

Othello recovers, and Iago tells him that Cassio will soon return. He will get Cassio to talk about his relationship with Desdemona, while Othello can hide and listen to this conversation, to which Othello agrees. It is rather Iago who gives Othello orders now, and not the other way around. While Othello is hiding, Iago reveals his plan to talk about Bianca with Cassio, knowing that this will cause his laughter and vex Othello, who will misinterpret Cassio's facial expressions and mistakenly believe that they are referring to Desdemona. When Cassio returns, the situation plays out exactly as Iago has imagined it with Othello furiously commenting on matters from his hiding-place. Cassio makes nasty remarks about Bianca and ridicules her affectionate behaviour.

Then Bianca herself arrives and hands Desdemona's handkerchief back to Cassio, refusing to copy the embroidery of it because she does not want to work on *some [other] minx's token* (l. 145). When she leaves, Cassio follows her to pacify her. Othello is convinced that he has seen Desdemona's handkerchief and therefore the proof of her unfaithfulness, although he also remembers how kind and beautiful his wife is. Eventually, he orders Iago to procure poison, but Iago callously suggests that he suffocate her with a cushion on their marriage bed, which she has *contaminated* (l. 194).

When Desdemona appears together with Lodovico, an envoy from Venice, the latter hands Othello a letter from the senate of Venice. The duke commands Othello to return to Venice and to appoint Cassio as Governor of Cyprus. When Desdemona, reporting to Lodovico that Othello and Cassio had a 'falling-out', shows her contentment about this outcome, Othello cries out in desperation. To the amazement of everyone present, he hits her in the face and sends her out. Desdemona says *I have not deserved this.* (l. 228) and weeps, but otherwise does not protest or ask for an explanation. Lodovico asks Othello to call her back, which he does, but also insults her as being immoral. Othello assures Lodovico that he will follow the given orders for his new commission and leaves. The Venetian envoy wonders if Othello has gone mad and Iago slyly implies that this might be so but advises Lodovico to draw his own conclusions.

What is the effect of Othello's epileptic fit on the audience?

Explain why Desdemona might be content about the orders from Venice.
Compare the way Desdemona and Bianca are treated by the men in this scene.
Bianca will not appear again in the play. What, in your view, is her function in scenes III, iv and IV, i?

Scene 2: In his jealous rage, Othello pressurises Emilia for evidence of his wife's unfaithfulness, but Emilia defends her mistress' loyalty with vigour. Emilia swears that she has never been witness to any wrongdoing by Desdemona when Cassio was present. All this, however, is of no avail, because Othello does not believe her and thinks her to be an accomplice in his wife's betrayal. When Desdemona comes, he brutally accuses her of falsehood and unfaithfulness, calling her a prostitute. Desdemona is desperate and implores him to trust her and believe in her innocence and fidelity (*'Upon my knees, what doth your speech import?'*, l. 30). This makes Othello even angrier, he ignores her pleas and leaves in a rage (*'would thou hadst ne'er been born'*, l. 68). Desdemona asks Emilia to fetch Iago and in her despair begs him to assure her husband that she is in no way the whore he thinks she is. She still believes that Othello's abominable behaviour towards her has its cause in the news from Venice. Emilia correctly suspects some involvement of an *'eternal villain'* (l. 129), who has poisoned Othello's mind, but has no inkling of her own husband's guilt. Iago says that Othello is preoccupied with matters of state. Still perplexed, Desdemona and Emilia go to supper.

Roderigo comes in, furiously complaining to Iago that all the gifts and precious stones he gave him to win Desdemona's favour so far have come to nothing and that he wants them returned. Otherwise he will disclose Iago's responsibility or challenge him to a duel. Iago diverts Roderigo by saying that he has been working for the latter's aim and promises that Desdemona will be available for him by the following night.

He lies that Othello will soon be posted to Mauritania, unless Cassio, the governor-to-be, meets with a fatal accident, which Roderigo needs to engineer. This way, Othello and Desdemona will stay in Cyprus. He tells Roderigo to meet him at Bianca's house at midnight where he will help him kill Cassio.

Point out the similarities and differences in the way Iago deals with Othello and Roderigo.
Compare Desdemona's and Emilia's reactions to Othello's reproaches.
Explain why so many characters think of Iago as 'honest' in spite of his numerous intrigues.

Scene 3: After dinner with their Venetian guests, Othello briskly orders Desdemona to go to bed and dismiss Emilia. Desdemona tells Emilia how much she still loves her husband despite his outrageous behaviour. She begs Emilia to use her wedding sheets as shrouds for her dead body should she die before her. After bed and nightclothes have been prepared, Desdemona touchingly sings a sad song of unhappy love she learnt from her mother's maid, Barbary, who died singing the *Willow Song* after her lover had left her. Desdemona says she finds Lodovico attractive and wants to know if Emilia would be unfaithful to her husband. The two women discuss men's fidelity in marriage, and Emilia admits that she would readily commit adultery if it helped her husband in his career, whereas Desdemona says she would never do this under any circumstances.

Being informed about the men's plans, the audience knows what will happen soon. Describe the atmosphere created in this scene and what function it has in this act.
Compare the different representations of jealousy witnessed in the play so far.

Act V

Scene 1: Positioned by Iago in a dark lane for an attack, Roderigo strikes out at Cassio when he comes by, but misses and is stabbed himself instead in the struggle. Unseen, Iago wounds Cassio in the leg and leaves. He would prefer both men to die, so that he could keep Roderigo's jewels and would not have to fear the exposure of his schemes through Cassio. Othello, who has overheard the brawl in hiding, believes Cassio has died and goes to kill his wife. Lodovico and Gratiano, Brabantio's brother, arrive and hesitate to investigate the scene for fear of being assaulted. Iago returns with a light and is recognised by the

Venetians towards whom he pretends ignorance of what happened. The wounded cry out loudly for help, and Iago 'finds' Cassio and claims that Roderigo was his attacker. While the Venetians look after Cassio, Iago stabs and kills Roderigo unnoticed. Bianca enters and is very distraught to find Cassio badly injured. To serve his own interests, Iago claims that she was involved in this fight, which Bianca denies. Emilia arrives and bawls at Bianca, calling her a prostitute, but Bianca refutes this vigorously. While Cassio is carried off in a chair for treatment and Roderigo's body is removed, Iago sends Emilia to inform Othello of the fight. In an aside, he says in the last sentence of this scene *'This is the night that either makes me or fordoes me quite.'* (ll. 128–129).

Compare the differences in atmosphere and tempo in IV, iii and V, i and explain their function.
Explain what Iago's last sentence means.

Scene 2: While Desdemona is asleep in bed, Othello reasons with himself why she must die. He kisses her and is almost moved to let her live, but then decides against it, because *'else she'll betray more men'* (l. 6). When she wakes up, he tells her to confess her sins before she dies. Aware of what is going to happen, she pleads for her life and denies that she has slept with Cassio or given him the handkerchief. Othello tells her that Iago has killed Cassio, whom he has also seen with the handkerchief and who boasted of having had sex with her. When Desdemona weeps, Othello takes this as a further confirmation of her guilt and love for Cassio. Despite her protestations and pleas for a delay, Othello mercilessly smothers her with a pillow, being absolutely convinced that she and Cassio both betrayed him. During all this, Emilia has knocked on the door, asking to be let in urgently. Othello pulls the curtain around the bed to hide his wife. When Emilia tells him that Roderigo is dead, and not Cassio, Othello is shocked. In one last desperate effort against dying, Desdemona raises her head, at first saying she was murdered, but then blaming herself for her own death before she passes away. Emilia is horrified to find her mistress dead, but does not suspect Othello of the deed. He calls Desdemona a liar and tells Emilia he killed her for deceiving him, of which he has sufficient proof from Iago. But Emilia does not believe one word of it and suspects her husband of having tricked Othello into believing this. She cries out loudly for everyone to hear that Othello has killed her mistress. Montano, Gratiano and Iago enter and Othello once more confirms what he has done. Gratiano says he is glad Brabantio will never know this, because he already died of grief following Desdemona's marriage. Despite Iago's attempts to silence her, Emilia asks him about his role in the matter and begins to understand Iago's unbelievably malicious deeds, who disputes this with *'I told him what I thought, and told no more than what he found himself was apt and true.'* (ll. 174–175). She tells Othello she took the handkerchief and gave it to Iago, and that Desdemona was completely innocent. Othello tries to attack Iago but is disarmed by Montano. To punish and finally silence Emilia, Iago stabs her from behind and flees. Gratiano stands guard outside, while Othello remains in the room with his dead wife and the dying Emilia and searches for another weapon. Having been overwhelmed by Montano and Lodovico, Iago is arrested and brought back for a trial and due punishment. Cassio is carried in as well. Othello tries to stab Iago a second time but only manages to wound him. When he asks him why he deceived him, Iago remains silent and refuses to say anything.

Lodovico and Cassio have found incriminating letters in dead Roderigo's possessions, and the full extent of Iago's pernicious plotting becomes obvious. In addition, Cassio tells Othello how he came by the handkerchief.

Lodovico orders Othello to give up his command and return to Venice with him, while Cassio will become the Governor of Cyprus and supervise Iago's torture and punishment.

Now fully aware of his monumental error in judgement, that he has killed his truly innocent wife and that there is no other way open for him than to follow her swiftly, Othello turns the weapon upon himself to be his own executioner. Before committing suicide, however, he tries to justify the premeditated murder of his wife, speaking remorsefully of himself as *'one that loved not wisely but too well'* (l. 340). He also underlines his loyalty to the Venetian state. Giving Desdemona a last kiss, he dies next to her. Lodovico awards Othello's property to Gratiano and leaves for Venice to report on the happenings.

Compare the three women's characters in terms of courage and independent behaviour.

Iago's deeds are out of proportion to his motives for them, which some critics have called 'motiveless malignancy' (= being evil). Can you agree with this statement?

Explain why Othello is a tragic figure.

Taking Othello's actions, feelings and mental state into account, can you agree with his opinion that he 'loved not wisely but too well'?

In your view, does the play have a satisfying ending?

The Characters

Othello

Many of Shakespeare's contemporaries were prejudiced against dark-skinned foreigners and their representation on stage was stereotypical: they were shown as overly emotional, simple, violent and lustful. Othello is the first black character with a convincing personality that does not reflect this racial bias. When Othello ends up behaving like the racist image others painted of him, it is due to his antagonist Iago's moral responsibility that this happened at all. Othello's lack of trust in his wife, his insecurities over his race and age as well as gullibility lead to his jealous rage and downfall, not the fact that he is a 'Moor'. This hero's tragic flaw is thereby universal and can serve as a warning for all the viewers. Othello's convincing remorse for Desdemona's murder, his attempt to kill the culprit Iago and his self-inflicted execution due to a feeling of repentance are pictured with pity for the character.

In the first act, where Venetian attitudes towards race are shown by Iago, Roderigo and Brabantio, whose daughter Desdemona Othello has secretly married, the racist caricature is presented (e.g. Iago: *'an old black ram is tupping your white ewe'*, I, i, ll. 89–90; Roderigo: *'thick-lips'*, I, i, l. 67; *'lascivious Moor'*, l. 125; Brabantio: *'sooty bosom of such a thing as thou'*, I, ii, ll. 70–71). However, when Othello appears in person in I, 2, his natural authority and his speeches suggest a dignified man with a successful military career and a healthy self-image. In spite of Brabantio and Roderigo's insults and threats, Othello remains calm and is convinced that the Duke of Venice will not take action against his general who has served the Venetian state so well as a mercenary soldier. Having a clear conscience and Desdemona's consent, Othello does not avoid a confrontation and is ready to take the matter before the Duke of Venice.

Shakespeare emphasises Othello's noble birth (I, ii, ll. 21–22) and gives him a colourful backstory full of adventures and proof of soldierly valour which Desdemona and her father admired when he repeatedly came to their house as a guest (I, iii, ll. 127–169). The fact that Desdemona chose to defy her society's expectations to marry the much older Othello does not only prove her courage, but also her strong belief in his *'honour and his valiant parts'* (I, iii, l. 249). The duke is full of praise for Othello as well, calling him *'valiant'* (I, iii, l. 48) and *'far more fair than black'* (I, iii, l. 286). Apart from that, Othello seems to be the only man fitting for this dangerous expedition which he accepts willingly and without delay. In Cyprus, Othello acts with authority as the new governor in wartimes and is not met with prejudice by anyone, nor is his interracial marriage commented upon negatively. In II, 1, the acting governor, Montano, speaks highly of Othello and his leadership (II, i, l. 30; ll. 34–40). Othello, once the threat of a hostile invasion is over, sees to his duties and gives the necessary orders. He has a herald proclaim general festivities to celebrate the destruction of the Turkish fleet and his wedding (II, 2). Since he commands Cassio and Iago to be on guard and not to indulge themselves, he demotes Cassio for his misconduct while on duty (III, 1) and inspects the battlements (III, 2). From III, 3 on, Iago can prey on Othello's mind as no urgent official duties must be carried out.

Up to this point, Othello has shown nothing but devotion to his wife, which he expresses tenderly (cf. 'Comparison of relationships' in this section, p. 60). In I, 3 he says *'My life upon her faith!'* (l. 290) when Brabantio warns him of her possibly deceiving him. Arriving in Cyprus, he is overjoyed to meet Desdemona after the stormy passage: *'O my soul's joy!'* (II, i, l. 177), *'If I were now to die, 'twere now to be most happy [...].'* (ll. 182–183) and *'I cannot speak enough of this content; it stops me here; it is of too much joy [...]!'* (ll. 189–190).

From a loving husband Othello changes into his wife's vindictive killer who morally disintegrates and shows signs of raving lunacy. The intensity of his jealous rage is so great that he even falls into a trance or has an epileptic seizure brought on by overexcitement or hypersensitivity. His suffering is shared by the audience who are fully aware of his misconception and wonder why he believes Iago rather than his wife. The two soldiers spent years together in combat, which must have intensified Othello's trust in Iago's integrity. He, a stranger to Venice, also takes for granted what Iago says about Venetian wives, who are rumoured to enjoy extramarital affairs. In addition, Iago sows doubt in Othello's mind by reminding him of Desdemona's deception of Brabantio (in which Othello was implicated, too, after all). Some critics believe that Othello is somewhat simple-minded, a doer rather than a thinker, and proficient in practical army matters, but not experienced or perceptive enough where other countries' cultures and morals are concerned. It is not easy to be a match for Iago, though. Other characters are as credulous as Othello is, because Iago is such a quick-thinking mastermind and successfully hiding his true nature until the very end. Iago certainly knows about Othello's insecurities as a black foreigner and outsider in Venice's prejudiced society and plays on them expertly (Othello's soliloquy, III, iii, ll. 259–278). He does not appreciate Desdemona's decision to oppose Venetian society for Othello's sake and ignores the fact that she has shown nothing but devotion for him.

As Othello loves Desdemona so deeply, he is also especially vulnerable to the vivid images of Desdemona's alleged sexual intercourse with Cassio that Iago plants in his mind, or to her giving away Othello's first gift, the handkerchief endowed with special magic powers. After his fit, Othello has totally adopted Iago's malicious intent as well as his way of speaking about her with contempt. Now he sees Desdemona and Cassio's death as the only solution to relieve himself of his painful passion. At the end of III, 3, he vows to kill them in a highly theatrical moment, in which Iago joins him, whose reward is his promotion to lieutenant.

After the so-called 'Temptation scene' (III, 3), Othello has lost all the love he felt for his wife and only seeks hard evidence for Iago's allegations. After eavesdropping on Iago and Cassio's talk staged by Iago as well as Cassio and Bianca's conversation during which the handkerchief is handed back by Bianca, Othello is absolutely convinced of Desdemona's guilt. He desperately needs to defend his male honour she has called into question by supposedly being disloyal and making him a cuckold. In act IV, Othello slanders Desdemona and Emilia, accusing them of being whores and a brothel-keeper and disregarding their vigorous protest. He strikes his wife in front of a delegation from Venice, who watch his transformation from the noble man they knew into a brutal savage in horror. The duke gave orders for Othello to return to Venice and for Cassio to become the new Governor of Cyprus. Desdemona, who is glad to hear this, because it means an end to the two men's disagreement, enrages Othello unintentionally because he interprets her contentment as an unspoken confession of her love for Cassio. In scene V, 1, during the street fight, Othello again merely overhears what happens and draws the wrong conclusion that Iago has indeed killed Cassio as he has sworn to do. Satisfied, Othello leaves to murder his wife. Even though he has moments in which he recalls his love for Desdemona or praises her beauty, Othello never trusts his younger wife enough to actively find out whether her pleas of innocence are truthful, nor does he have any doubt about Iago's allegations. When watching the sleeping Desdemona in V, 2, Othello admires her and contemplates his purpose again, but then coolly decides to end her life *'else she'll betray more men'* (V, ii, l. 6). Earlier, he determined to kill her with poison in order not to be disarmed by her charms (IV, i, ll. 190–192) and now decides to make her death as painless as possible (V, ii, l. 89). He checks repeatedly whether she has said her prayers so that her soul can go to heaven. Only now does he confront Desdemona with his full charge against her and inform her of Cassio's demise. He mistakes Desdemona's shock at Cassio's death as further proof of her feelings for him, and this spurs him on to commit the crime. Immune to her entreaty to spare her or delay his intended deed, Othello mercilessly smothers her with a pillow on their wedding bed, turning it into a tomb. In the brief moment of consciousness before she finally dies, Desdemona blames herself for her death in front of Emilia. Othello scoffs at this, calling her a liar and corrects his wife as to who the perpetrator was. He is still convinced of being in the right when he meets the men Emilia alerted to his deed. During the time it takes to explain Iago's involvement and when other characters corroborate the witnesses' statements, Othello experiences genuine grief over what he has done (V, ii, ll. 270–279). He fails to kill Iago in revenge twice, is stripped of his rank and ordered to return to Venice with Lodovico, the duke's envoy. Iago leaves Othello without any explanation of his motives. At the end, before he chooses to be his own executioner, Othello stresses his loyalty to Venice. In his last speech, he compares himself to a Turk whom he killed for beating a Venetian and for berating the state of Venice and indirectly admits that he himself, as a Christian, sinned against the commandments of the Church and acted contrary to the code of honour befitting a high-ranking soldier. He himself, after having realised his fundamental error, fully accepts his destiny in hell, which religion has laid down for sinners. In his case, he is doubly damned, firstly as a murderer and secondly as a suicide.

Othello's own estimate that he *'loved not wisely but too well'* (V, ii, l. 340) will not ring true to the audience or the other characters present, but his self-inflicted punishment gives him back some stature. His image is extremely important to him, to the extent that he wants to define how he is remembered before he commits suicide. Had he been charged in Venice, he would have been found guilty of premeditated murder and be condemned to death. He planned Desdemona's murder beforehand and showed no repentance until he learned of his error. Othello allowed emotion to dominate over rational thinking and proper moral conduct.

In a medieval Morality Play, his character would be that of a human soul placed between an angel and the devil who would both fight hard for his loyalty. After having been tempted and sinned, he would be forgiven and shown mercy, like Desdemona does in the play.

Iago

Shakespeare chose to call his villain after the patron saint of England's archenemy, Spain, 'Sant' Iago' or Saint James the Greater, whose byname is 'Matamoros' or 'the Moor-Slayer'.

Iago, Othello's flag-bearer, sets out to destroy Othello's happiness by convincing him that his wife Desdemona has an affair with the general's lieutenant Cassio. Iago's numerous acts of malice seem disproportionate to the motives he offers for them, since four characters are dead at the end of the play.

From the first scene onward, Iago explains his intentions and shares his schemes with the audience. He has recruited Desdemona's jilted lover Roderigo to do the dirty work for him and leads him to believe that all is done to win Desdemona's favour for Roderigo. In Iago's soliloquies, his true motives are disclosed: Firstly, he was passed over for promotion in favour of Cassio, whom he thinks hardly suitable for this position (I, i, ll. 19–27). Iago points out that he and Othello have fought together in many battles, in which Iago has proved himself worthy (I, i, ll. 28–31). Thus, Iago feels slighted and perceives Othello as an unfair superior who disregards years of service and loyalty. Secondly, he suspects both Othello and Cassio of having betrayed him with his wife Emilia and seeks revenge for this, although he does not show much of overt jealousy. When provoking other men's anger or jealousy, Iago uses explicit images of sex coming from his active, possibly jealous, imagination (*'an old black ram is tupping your white ewe'* to anger Brabantio, (I, i, ll. 89–90) and his description of Cassio supposedly dreaming of Desdemona (III, iii, ll. 414–427).

There does not seem to be much in Iago's life that indicates emotional or marital satisfaction, and he reduces all love to sex. He draws pleasure only from his superior intellect by playing mind-games, which might make him envious of others' richer emotional lives. In V, i, ll. 19–20 he says about Cassio, who seems to enjoy life and is welcome where he goes: *'He hath a daily beauty in his life that makes me ugly [...]'.* Despite his confessed hatred for 'the Moor', Iago concedes that Othello has a *'constant, noble, loving nature'* who will *'prove to Desdemona a most dear husband'* (II, i, ll. 271–272). He feels contempt for Othello's *'free and open nature, that thinks men honest that but seem to be so'* (I, iii, ll. 379–380), because Othello is so easily led by him, but on the other hand, Iago also seems to envy his virtuous qualities. Outwardly, he scorns deep-felt emotions in an arrogant manner.

In contrast, Iago has a very low opinion of Roderigo, calling him a *'fool'* (I, iii, l. 363), *'such a snipe'* (I, iii, l. 365) and *'this poor trash of Venice'* (II, i, l. 284), but does not tire of encouraging him further and of lying to him in order to follow his plans through. Iago only fills his life with destructive energy directed against other people's success or happiness. His relationship with his wife is not happy either, which he refers to when he talks about her nagging him (II, i, ll. 100–102) or about his suspicion that she has slept with other men. Iago makes his wife an unwitting accomplice but does not foresee her readiness to serve justice and the greater good rather than to protect him. Coming close to unveiling his part in rousing Othello's jealousy in IV, 2, Emilia fully exposes her husband's guilt in V, 2, for which he stabs her in retaliation. Hers is the second murder he commits after killing Roderigo in V, 1 simply to avoid being found out.

His character has been compared to the medieval stereotype of 'Vice', a representation of the tempting devil leading human beings astray and imbuing them with ill nature. Iago seems to have no other quality than being evil for evil's sake, which prompted critics to call his ambitions 'motiveless malignity'.

Another theory attempting to explain Iago's motives is that he might be in love with Othello and therefore want to wreck his marriage. There is little evidence of Iago feeling anything like empathy, affection or true love for anyone. In the process of destroying Othello's marriage, Iago would not automatically engender Othello's love. Since Iago often comments on Othello in a disparaging way, there is little probability for such a motive. Iago's views on women could be called misogynistic, as he often expresses his contempt, and calls them generally deceitful and sex-starved (II, i, ll. 108–114). He takes delight in his own cleverness, gloating over Othello's anguish ('*Work on, my medicine, work!*', IV, i, ll. 42–43) and uses irony in his soliloquies: '*And what's he then that says I play the villain?*' (II, iii, l. 307). Iago can think on his feet and exploit everything that fits in with his plotting but is also lucky that these opportunities arise.

The list of Iago's lies and deceptions is long: In act I, he announces he will continue in Othello's service only to serve his own interests and incites Roderigo to inform Brabantio of his daughter's escape while staying incognito himself. He pretends loyalty to Othello but informs the search party where they can find the runaways. Unashamedly, he makes Roderigo an accomplice and uses his money for his own purposes. To involve both his enemies Othello and Cassio in his schemes, he will hint that Cassio is too familiar with Desdemona. In act II, in Cyprus, Iago uses his knowledge of Cassio's low tolerance for alcohol to get him drunk and sets Roderigo up to fight him. He falsely informs Montano that Cassio has a drinking problem to blacken his reputation and has Roderigo alert the town to the brawl in the guards' room. When asked to report on what took place, Iago seemingly defends Cassio while slandering and incriminating him. In the 'Temptation scene', III, 3, Iago entirely convinces Othello that his wife is unfaithful and must be killed in retribution.

He insinuates that Cassio, enlisting Desdemona's help to gain his position back, has a guilty conscience when he departs the same moment Othello arrives. Iago asks leading questions that hint at Cassio not being honest in his role as go-between during Othello's courtship with Desdemona. Pretending he would rather not share his thoughts, Iago entices Othello to press him to speak out. He warns Othello not to be jealous while encouraging it simultaneously and drops hints at Desdemona's lacking fidelity. Having implicated Emilia in his intrigues, he grabs the handkerchief she picked up and will drop it in Cassio's lodgings to have evidence for adultery. When Othello is convinced of Desdemona's disloyalty, Iago goads him on, working upon the furious Othello to intensify his rage with false accusations and graphic images of a sexual nature (Cassio's dream). Iago lies in that he has seen Cassio wiping his beard with the handkerchief that he must still have in his pocket. Finally, Iago is made lieutenant by Othello, swears loyalty to him and vows to kill Cassio. This moment marks the absolute triumph for Iago's self-esteem and he says: '*I am your own for ever.*' (III, iii, l. 480). How much truth lies in these words is open to question – it might just have been said with Iago's ulterior motive to give thanks for the promotion, but considering their earlier comradeship, there is perhaps a hint of the relationship they had. In a more sinister interpretation, Iago might also refer to being a devastating influence Othello cannot get rid of.

In act IV, Iago continues his incrimination of Desdemona and pretends that kissing and sleeping with another man is innocent simply in order to kindle Othello's rage even further. He lies when telling that Cassio brags of having slept with Desdemona and stages a talk with Cassio for Othello to overhear that seems to be about Desdemona.

When the envoys from Venice are amazed to witness Othello's unhinged behaviour, Iago feigns reluctance to criticise Othello, but indirectly warns Lodovico that he might not have seen the worst regarding Othello's change. Breaking his vow to Othello, Iago plots Cassio's death by Roderigo's hand and hides while urging Roderigo to attack Cassio in V, 1. Unseen, he stabs Cassio in the leg when Roderigo has failed his mission and ruthlessly kills Roderigo to get rid of his witness. In V, 2, after Emilia has told the truth about the handkerchief, he denies her allegations and then cowardly stabs her from behind and flees. Letters found in Roderigo's property, a confession of complicity before his death and Cassio's testimony, give full insight into Iago's machinations – he himself admits only to have dropped the handkerchief into Cassio's room (V, ii, ll. 318–320). Iago does not explain his motives to Othello, who tries to kill him twice, and announces his intention to keep silent from this moment on after having imparted so much during the whole play. Othello calls him a '*demi-devil*' (V, ii, l. 298) and indeed, although Shakespeare's contemporaries associated the colour black with the devil, the most diabolical character in the play is not Othello but white Iago.

Iago swears by Janus, the two-faced Roman god (I, i, l. 33) and thus shows himself to be the hypocrite associated with this deity. He is perceptive enough to prey on other characters' insecurities and deficiencies and enjoys manipulating and corrupting them skilfully with his dishonesty and immoral opportunism.

Modern psychology would call him an unscrupulous narcissist and vindictive sociopath who turns into a cold-blooded serial murderer to cover his tracks.

Why nobody suspects 'honest' Iago

Apparently, people have not been deceived by Iago before, as his resentment only began when he did not get the position of lieutenant. Others therefore have not known him as malicious, revengeful or two-faced.

Roderigo is the only one who could reveal Iago's schemes, but Iago controls him completely and can incite him to commit dangerous or potentially lethal deeds like sword fights. Even after Roderigo's refusal to comply with Iago's requests any longer and his threat of exposure, Iago quickly has him back on track.

His wife Emilia accepts getting no reply when she asks him what he intends to do with the handkerchief and fears no real mischief. When she believes a villain responsible for Othello's jealousy, she does not think of Iago as the culprit. Every time when Iago incriminates other characters in front of Othello, he does so hesitatingly, pretending to see their good sides or condoning their faults, even begging Othello to be lenient or to reconsider his decisions, which allows Iago to appear as a decent, honourable and not self-serving man.

Othello, Cassio, Desdemona and Roderigo all ask Iago for advice, which he gives in such a manner that it is acceptable or reassuring. They are grateful and heed it, even if not everyone is totally convinced, like Roderigo for instance. Iago thus plays the mischievous double role of the villain and the trustworthy friend.

How audiences feel about Iago

From the beginning, the viewers know Iago is not as honest as everyone else believes (*'I am not what I am'*, I, 1, l. 66) and become unwilling co-conspirators to his plots. They feel awkward to watch the results of his intrigues and might have compassion for his clueless victims, maybe hoping that the anticipated deeds will not happen or Iago's plans will be averted in time. Watching the plot unfold, the audience thus experiences suspense, wondering also how the plots will work out. While the tragic actions of murder and suicide are acted out on stage, they might feel horror at such senseless destruction for which only one evil-minded individual is responsible. At the same time, the spectators might admire Iago's high intelligence and impressive skills of manoeuvring others around, like a theatre director blocking actors on stage. At any rate, Iago has successfully demonstrated the power of evil which played on his victim's insecurities and weaknesses and taught the audience one of the lessons of tragedy by instilling fear in them.

Desdemona

Many critics see Desdemona more as a personification of Christian values worth striving for than as a fully rounded character that also possesses negative qualities. In medieval plays, she would have represented an angel or would have played the part of 'Virtue', whose unconditional, spiritual love and forgiveness even lead to self-sacrifice and the full acceptance of God's will. Her inherent and constant goodness defies the villain's intrigues and triumphs over evil with a martyr-like resignation at the cost of her life.

Senator Brabantio, her father, describes her as never 'bold', a quiet spirit, introverted and bashful, afraid of people like Othello and a virtuous, innocent girl obedient to him. He errs in this assumption, though, as she secretly elopes and marries a man her Venetian social environment is deeply biased against. She rejected all Venetian suitors but was conquered by Othello's wondrous tales and let him know indirectly that she would accept a proposal of marriage from him. According to Brabantio, she has committed an unheard-of act of rebellion against all propriety and thrown away her beauty, intelligence and honour for a dark-skinned stranger when she could have chosen among many worthy Venetians. When interrogated about her choice in I, 3, Desdemona is respectful and acknowledges her father's role and position in society so far but sees her duty of obedience now transferred to her husband, cleverly comparing herself to her mother. In this moment of the play, she is portrayed as a self-possessed, independent, intelligent woman who follows her heart, asserts her will, defies her society's prejudices, refuses to return to Brabantio's house and is willing to face the consequences.

Desdemona also expresses her deep love for Othello and insists on accompanying him to Cyprus.

Up to III, 3, Desdemona and Othello display deeply felt mutual love for each other, using terms of endearment and speaking about each other full of respect and admiration (cf. 'Comparison of relationships' in this section, p. 60). He often refers to her beauty and kindness, and all the male protagonists are attracted to her, too. In Othello's report on their courtship in I, 3, it becomes obvious though that it is rather affection and compassion than passionate, romantic love which connects the older man with his young wife ('*She loved me for the dangers I had passed, and I loved her that she did pity them.*', I, iii, ll. 166–167). While waiting for Othello's ship to land in Cyprus, Desdemona banters with Iago, showing her intelligence and good breeding. When asked for help by Cassio, she undertakes this task very earnestly, even saying she will '*rather die than give thy cause away*' (III, iii, ll. 27–28), and pleads for Cassio as soon as Othello appears, reminding her husband of Cassio's role as go-between in their courtship and insisting that it is no small matter when he seems reluctant to discuss the case. Desdemona's lobbying for Cassio shows her good nature, though she maybe presses the matter too much and distracts Othello with the request when she is embarrassed to tell him that she lost the handkerchief her husband gave her. Iago's description of her character, even if used to persuade Cassio that he should ask her for assistance, is very fitting: '*[…] she is of so free, so kind, so apt, so blessed a disposition, she holds it a vice in her goodness not to do more than she is requested […].*' (II, iii, ll.

293–295). Desdemona's love for Othello never wavers, even when he is ill-tempered, strikes her or calls her a whore. She says '*I have not deserved this.*' (IV, i, l. 228) and weeps, but does not criticise or retaliate against Othello or ask why he has done this and leaves when he rages at her. She worries more about what ails him than feeling indignation or anger at his treatment of her. '*my love doth so approve him, that even his stubbornness, his checks, his frowns [...] have grace and favour to them*' (IV, iii, ll. 18–20). Emilia's suggestion that Othello might be jealous does not convince her, since she knows that she gave him no reason for it, and she ascribes his aggression to his recall to Venice or to state matters. Unintentionally, she worsens her own situation and kindles Othello's jealousy further, when she hopes for a reconciliation between the two men ('*for the love I bear Cassio*', IV, i, l. 218). She is also glad that Cassio will become Governor of Cyprus, which makes any further pleading with Othello on behalf of Cassio superfluous. Othello understands Desdemona's remarks as further proof of an intimate relationship with Cassio and of her being content with the latter's achievement in spite of Othello's decision to dismiss Cassio. His words '*Are you wise?*' and '*Devil!*' (IV, i, ll. 221; 227) underline this interpretation. When Othello tells her that Cassio is dead in V, 2, she weeps and says '*Alas! He is betrayed and I undone.*' (V, ii, l. 77), which Othello wrongly interprets as a confirmation of their guilt. Desdemona's steadfast and unswerving loyalty, which is also emphasised by her inability to imagine adultery for herself (IV, iii, ll. 62; 74–75), forms a stark contrast to Iago's slander and Othello's unjust reproaches concerning her fidelity.

Desdemona's resignation to her undeserved death has frustrated many viewers, particularly when she revives for a moment from her deathbed to exonerate Othello from his crime and asks Emilia to '*commend [her] to [her] kind lord*' (V, ii, l. 125). Her motive might have been to spare her murderer his punishment, who moments later boasts of his deed and calls his wife a 'liar'. For her time and considering the constraints women were exposed to, she is a model wife who obeys her husband and suffers his outbursts, reproaches and finally murderous deed. A more critical and modern interpretation might see Desdemona as unwise in her unwavering love for Othello, pitiful in her simple innocence, pathetic in her lacking instincts, too passive and fatalistic and victimised by a wife-batterer and murderer. There is little left of her braver stance from the beginning, when she stood up against Brabantio and defended her marriage.

Emilia

Iago's wife is Desdemona's attendant, who feels loyalty and affection for her mistress, although she is unaware of her decisive role in providing the handkerchief her husband will use to prove Desdemona's alleged unfaithfulness to Othello. Emilia shows Iago the handkerchief she picked up from the floor, but senses no malice when he grabs it from her, offering no explanation. However, she fails to tell Desdemona the truth about its whereabouts, when her mistress looks for it and worries. Emilia is helpful and reports how matters stand when Cassio comes to talk to Desdemona about his reinstatement. Her marriage to Iago seems loveless with no exchanges of mutual affection and her enduring his insults (II, i, ll. 100–102). Alone with Desdemona, Emilia speaks condescendingly about men and marriage (IV, iii, ll. 80–99), and, in contrast to her mistress, can imagine having an adulterous affair when it serves Iago's career. She is the only one who detects the true reason for Othello's furious outbursts and violent reactions, who only treats her as if she were a brothel-keeper and ignores her protestations that Desdemona is faithful to him. Coming close to detecting her husband's plotting, Emilia assumes that *'some eternal villain'* seeking advancement has poisoned Othello's mind (IV, ii, ll. 129–132). Emilia is sharp-tongued, direct and more worldly than the young and innocent Desdemona. She is a voice of common sense and has the function of an older sister or mother, though Desdemona does not heed her advice. Her greatest moment in the play occurs in V, 2, when she denounces Othello as a murderer and insults him, risking her own safety, as he might assault her, too. Due to her belated honesty concerning the handkerchief, Iago's involvement in Desdemona's death becomes apparent, a fact which enrages Emilia greatly. She is appalled when the full extent of Iago's machinations is discovered and says *'My husband!'* four times in disbelief and realises how wrong she was about him. In spite of her cleverness, she has misjudged Iago and now refuses to obey him: *'Tis proper I obey him, but not now. Perchance,*

Iago, I will ne'er go home.' (V, ii, ll. 194–195). Transferring her loyalty now completely to her dead mistress, she disregards Iago's warnings to be silent and exposes his schemes for which he cold-bloodedly stabs her in reprisal. Her last sentence again confirms Desdemona's innocence before Emilia dies next to her. Both women were unjustly scorned, punished and died at their own husbands' hands and are thus foils to each other.

Cassio

He is Othello's newly appointed lieutenant and second-in-command, who, according to Iago, does not deserve this promotion because he considers him lacking in military expertise and experience. Michael Cassio is a handsome and well-bred Florentine gentleman with courteous manners, who trusts in his charm and effect on women. He was also a go-between during Othello's and Desdemona's courtship. Iago describes Cassio to Roderigo in a spiteful way (II, i, ll. 227–235) to enlist help for his own revenge. He is envious of the promotion he wanted for himself and of Cassio's standing in Othello's esteem. Iago's remark *'He (Cassio) hath a daily beauty in his life that makes me ugly […].'* (V, i, ll. 19–20) reveals his hatred for the young man's happier disposition. After landing in Cyprus, Cassio expresses exaggerated reverence for Desdemona (II, i, ll. 61–65; 74–87), using high-flown language which shows his education, and is quite daring when kissing Emilia as his greeting in a *'bold show of courtesy'* (II, i, l. 99).

Since Cassio admitted that he has no tolerance for alcohol but has already drunk a cup, Iago gets him completely drunk and involves him in a fight with Roderigo. His rash and impulsive actions result in Cassio's being demoted for brawling while on guard duty. Iago then befriends Cassio, who is devastated by this loss of reputation and expresses his remorse exhaustively (*'O, I have lost my reputation! I have lost the immortal part of myself, and what remains is bestial. My reputation, Iago, my reputation!'* (II, iii, ll. 243–245 and ll. 255–260; ll. 265–269; 272–274). Unaware of Iago's duplicity, Cassio heeds his advice to engage Desdemona's help in his reinstatement.

He does not talk to Othello directly, but engages Emilia and Desdemona on his behalf and has musicians play to ingratiate himself in front of the castle.

Having persuaded Othello earlier that his wife and Cassio are lovers and even planting the handkerchief in Cassio's room, Iago manages to incriminate the blameless Cassio to the extent that Othello wants him killed by Iago. Cassio is lucky to survive Roderigo and Iago's orchestrated attempt on his life in V, 1, and he only fully understands the conspiracy after the villain has been exposed, and then testifies against him.

Cassio enjoys his relationship with Bianca, though he does not see her as often as she would like and pokes fun at her openly shown affection for him in front of Iago, who uses this conversation in order to enrage the eavesdropping Othello. When Iago suggests a marriage to Bianca, Cassio laughs mockingly, which shows his disdain for their affair. He still cares for her enough to mollify her when she jealously rails at him, runs after her and even has dinner with her at her house. At the end of the play, Cassio is shocked when he discovers Othello's suspicion against him. He regains his dignity when he is named Governor of Cyprus, who is entitled to enforce Iago's torture and punishment.

Roderigo

Suffering from unrequited love for Desdemona, the Venetian gentleman Roderigo still tries to win her affections in spite of her devotion to her husband Othello. When Roderigo, instigated by Iago, alerts Desdemona's father Brabantio to her flight, it becomes clear that his wooing was not welcome (I, i, ll. 97–102). He is preferable to Othello, though (I, i, l. 174), whom Roderigo reviles with racial epithets (*'thick-lips'*, I, i, l. 67; *'lascivious Moor'*, l. 125). From the beginning, it is clear to the audience how extensively Roderigo is duped by Iago, although he believes Iago to be his go-between in his planned seduction of Othello's wife. Iago thinks very little of Roderigo, whom he calls a *'fool'* (I, iii, 363), *'such a snipe'* (I, iii, l. 365) and *'this poor trash of Venice'* (II, i, l. 284). Roderigo is ready to travel to Cyprus and invest precious jewels and all of his money for this purpose, which he foolishly hands over to Iago in spite of lacking visible progress in the undertaking. When Roderigo complains about this, Iago quickly and easily manages to give plausible reasons for the alleged delays and obstacles, and ropes him in again (IV, ii, ll. 172–234). Iago can convince Roderigo that Desdemona will soon tire of Othello and prefer Roderigo as a younger lover (I, iii, ll. 338–340), that Iago will be loyal to him (I, iii, l. 349), that Desdemona is in love with Cassio (II, i, ll. 235–248) and that she will be available for him when Cassio is dead (IV, ii, ll. 208–210).

It is surprising to what extent the villain Iago can exploit Roderigo to assist him in his schemes: he is ready to provoke a fight with Cassio to ruin his prospects in order to get Desdemona's supposed lover out of the way, raise a general alarm in Cyprus (II, iii, ll. 120–139) and finally even to ambush and kill Cassio in V, 1.

Roderigo can be described as gullible, easily led and feeble-minded as he does what Iago tells him to do and never sticks to his own short-lived protestations. His emotional states range from being lovesick to maudlin and melodramatic when he speaks of drowning himself (I, iii, l. 301), but Iago can quickly dissuade him.

Roderigo seems spineless and immature when he sulks and 'whinges' like a child and never stands up to Iago in spite of his complaints, even after threatening Iago with a duel (IV, ii, ll. 192–195). Maybe he does suspect Iago of double-crossing him, because he writes down what Iago asked him to do and keeps the letters on his person. When they are found, Iago's conspiracy is accidentally confirmed. Although he does not want to attack Cassio, Roderigo does so anyway without any scruples and dies an unspectacular death when Iago stabs him, only then fully realising how consummately he was framed.

Roderigo's function is that of a likewise gullible foil to Othello who is deceived by Iago in the same way, though on a larger tragic scale. Roderigo's part advances the action and allows Iago's participation in the intrigue to remain unnoticed for a long time. Apart from that, the two murder plots are mirrored in Roderigo and Iago's plan to kill Cassio.

Brabantio

He is an old Venetian aristocrat and a senator in the duke's council, but the important conference on the expected Turkish attack on Cyprus takes place without him. Brabantio invited Othello often to hear his stories about his life and traveller's adventures, but when Desdemona runs away with him, he is horrified. He is especially outraged when thinking of his only child in Othello's arms (*'sooty bosom of such a thing as thou'*, I, ii, ll. 70–71), or, as suggested by Iago in I, 1, having sex with him. In I, 2, he accuses Othello of having used magic potions or spells and wants him arrested for witchcraft, which fails when his daughter testifies to her love for Othello before the Duke of Venice, whom Brabantio thought to be on his side. He has lost his honour because he could not control Desdemona and feels intense grief over her disobedience and choice of a husband (I, iii, ll. 187–196; ll. 208–218). Besides, his description of Desdemona in I, 3 as never 'bold', a quiet spirit, introverted and bashful, even afraid of foreigners like Othello, forms a stark contrast to the independence she shows when defending her actions.

Seeing that his protests are futile, Brabantio grudgingly gives the married couple a reluctant blessing. In a vindictive and sarcastic comment, he warns Othello that she might be disloyal to him, too, and does not want her to stay in his house anymore. In V, 2, his brother Gratiano reports that Brabantio's grief at Desdemona's action was so immense that he died of it.

Brabantio is the typical criticising parent figure who objects to his child's decision or assertion of its free will and represents the force of opposition a protagonist has to struggle with.

Brabantio's racial prejudice and hatred of Othello (*'foul thief'*, *'damned as thou art'*, *'sooty bosom of such a thing as thou'*, (I, ii, ll. 62; 63; 70–71) show the extent of Othello's isolation as an outsider in Venice.

The Duke of Venice

In I, 3, the duke is portrayed as a competent leader and fair ruler of the Venetian city state who sees through a strategic feint of the Turkish fleet and sends for Othello to defend Cyprus from an attack, which shows his trust in Othello's military skills and his ability to make appropriate political decisions. He has more pressing concerns than Brabantio's private sorrow but allows him to interrupt his council meeting all the same. Faced with Brabantio's accusations of Othello's apparent wrongdoing, he listens to both sides. He is not swayed by racial prejudice against Othello, understands why Desdemona fell in love with him and allows the couple to leave together for Cyprus, trying to reconcile all parties. The duke feels empathy for Brabantio's feelings as well and tries to raise Othello in his esteem (*'your son-in-law is far more fair than black'*, I, iii, l. 286) and console the irate father with proverb-like wisdom: *'To mourn a mischief that is past and gone, is the next way to draw more mischief on.'* (I, iii, ll. 202–203). Like Brabantio, the Duke of Venice only appears in the first act and serves as his foil: on the one hand, there is the interfering parent vetoing a child's choice of partner, while on the other hand the personified voice of reason condones the child's actions with his tolerant stance.

Bianca

She appears only briefly in three scenes (III, 4; IV, 1; V, 1), but Bianca's character is important in moving the plot forward as she is unwittingly implicated in Iago's scheming. Bianca is Cassio's mistress and has her own house in Cyprus where, according to Iago, she lives *'by selling her desires buys herself bread and clothes'* (IV, i, ll. 92–93). Emilia calls her a prostitute, too, though both have just arrived from Venice and are not familiar with the island's population. Bianca is greatly infatuated with Cassio and not afraid to show her affection publicly (Cassio: *'she haunts me in every place'*, IV, i, l. 128; *'falls me thus about my neck'*; *'so hangs, and lolls, and weeps upon me; so hales and pulls me'*, IV, i, ll. 130–134). Her genuine concern for him is obvious when she sees him severely wounded in V, 1 and is taken away for further questioning by Iago, who wants to incriminate her as a guilty party in the assault. Her relationship with Cassio might be one-sided, but her love and her jealous fury seem more rational than Othello's. She suspects Cassio of having another lover beside her who has given him the handkerchief whose embroidery he asked her to copy. Iago uses his own and Bianca's conversations with Cassio and her handing back the handkerchief in anger in order to fool Othello into wrongly concluding that his concerns about Desdemona's fidelity are justified. Bianca and Cassio's relationship can be seen as an echo of the main plot contrasting the two married Venetian couples.

Montano

Called a man of *'most allowed sufficiency'* (= competent) (I, iii, ll. 221–222) by the Duke of Venice, the acting Governor of Cyprus, Montano, is to be replaced by Othello, the experienced battle commander, when a Turkish invasion of Venice's colony is anticipated. Montano does not resent this order but declares this decision adequate and Othello worthy of the task (II, i, ll. 30; 34–40). In the brawl in II, 3, Montano is wounded by Cassio when he tries to interrupt his fight with Roderigo, but is sufficiently recovered in V, 2 when he disarms Othello and later chases and captures Iago. With Cassio's new appointment as governor, Montano's service ends, although he could have been reappointed.

Lodovico

Like his fellow traveller Gratiano, he only appears at the end of the play to deliver Othello's new brief and see to Cassio's inauguration as Cyprus' new governor. Lodovico is a relative of Brabantio and, very shocked at Desdemona's public shaming, asks Othello to call her back and make amends to her.

He represents the voice of reason and normality in the emotionally charged atmosphere of the play's last scenes. Reminding the audience of Othello's former even-tempered behaviour, he explicitly points at the enormity of the general's change, wondering about his sanity. Emilia and Desdemona agree that Lodovico is an attractive man, though he does not make use of it like Cassio. After Iago's arrest and Othello's suicide, he exerts authority and gives the necessary orders before he returns to Venice for an official report of the occurrences in Cyprus.

Gratiano

Brabantio's brother, Gratiano, only arrives at the close of the play to witness Othello's disintegration and inform the other characters in Cyprus of Brabantio's death because of the sorrow he felt at Desdemona's marriage. Asked to help along with Lodovico in the street fight in V, 1 and approached by Emilia in V, 2 after she has found Desdemona dead, Gratiano is not overly effectual in stopping neither Iago in his trickery nor Othello wielding weapons. He is the last remaining relative of Desdemona as well as the recipient of Othello's inheritance. Together with Lodovico, he is another representative of Venetian society.

Clown

Clowns or comic actors were often used in Elizabethan theatre companies to lighten the mood (even in tragedies). They were given extra parts and commonly used word plays. In *Othello*, the clown is a servant in Othello's household who sends off the musicians paid by Cassio, unable to resist making obscene jokes (III, 1). In III, 4, he carries a message for Desdemona, again jesting without adding much to the plot.

▶ **Points to remember:**
- Also called flat characters or stereotypes, minor characters have few qualities.
- They do not undergo a development during the play and do not appear often.
- Minor characters have a particular purpose in the play, e. g. to:
  ○ mirror a main character or serve as a foil to him
  ○ move the action forward (e.g. Bianca)
  ○ represent opposing forces a character has to struggle against (Brabantio)
  ○ represent the benevolent counterpart that helps a character (the Duke of Venice)

- represent the respective society and its values (Montano, Lodovico, Gratiano)
- provide comic relief and entertainment (Clown)

Comparison of characters

Who is the main protagonist?

Iago, as the play's villain, is given much space to allow an insight into his character and machinations. He has more lines and soliloquies than the titular character Othello and no real counterforce to struggle against. Iago dominates the first part and has carried out his intention at the end of III, 3, when both men vow to kill Desdemona and Cassio, while the focus in the second part of the play is on Othello. Iago never undergoes a development typical of a main character and has no inner life worth watching unlike that of Othello. Iago seems like a director pulling all of his actors' strings and preparing and supervising every move they make. However, he is also lucky and takes chances. In this scenario, Othello rather reacts to Iago's suggestions instead of taking action himself until the end of the play, where his violent outbursts and intense grief grab the audience's attention. Both characters are contrasted with each other: Othello is transparent and thinks all men are honest like himself, while Iago is duplicitous to the extreme. Othello's emotional journey through the play is far more dramatic and moving than Iago's intellectual strategies that serve as a warning for the audience not to fall victim to manipulators. Both are equally important to the play because one could not exist without the other.

The women

Both Desdemona and Emilia are innocent victims of male aggressiveness and are killed by their respective husbands: Othello kills his wife because he believes she betrayed him, whereas Iago stabs Emilia because she told the truth about his machinations. The women react differently towards their aggressors: Emilia affronts Othello and Iago in order to serve justice, confessing her implication in the theft of the handkerchief, while Desdemona does not fight at all. She pleads for her life in vain and is not even given the chance to prove her innocence. In her dying breath, at first, she protests she was murdered, but then shifts the blame onto herself to spare Othello the legal consequences and rightful punishment. This is a martyr-like devotion or forgiveness which is not easy to comprehend. Emilia defies her master who has just killed her mistress and she chooses to be loyal to Desdemona and to incriminate the real culprit, her husband Iago. Bianca's part is small but vital, as Iago uses her actions to weave his sinister web even further. The three women are foils to each other as they are so different in their age, social standing and behaviour, but they bear a striking similarity in that they all love a man who treats them badly and that their love makes them vulnerable. The handkerchief draws the women together, who are all unaware of the purpose it serves Iago.

Another resemblance is the way the men treat them. They show little respect for the women, use slander or impose their male fantasies on them or fear to lose their honour by being cuckolded. Desdemona is even struck, and both she and Emilia die at their husbands' hands.

Cassio makes nasty remarks about Bianca, though he is friendly with her when they are alone, and ridicules her affectionate behaviour. It is never clearly said whether she really is a prostitute or only called that by everyone. At any rate, Cassio is very adamant that he would never marry her. Iago vilifies women throughout the play. When Othello thinks of what a kind, delicate and beautiful person his wife is, Iago argues that such traits only hide her devious sexuality and threaten Othello's manhood. Othello has conflicting feelings for Desdemona but is so consumed by jealousy that his hatred and hurt pride win over the love he once felt for her.

Comparison of relationships

Without Iago's interference, Othello and Desdemona's relationship would have remained as happy as it was at the beginning of the play. Both express affection for each other when interrogated by Brabantio and the Duke of Venice and continue speaking in this way. Othello and Desdemona both use terms of endearment during their greetings and kiss when meeting in Cyprus in II, 1 (Othello: '*O my fair warrior!*', l. 175; '*O my soul's joy!*', l. 177; '*Honey*', l. 197; '*o my sweet*', l. 198; Desdemona: '*My dear Othello!*', l. 176). In II, 3, there are further examples: Othello: '*my dear love*', l. 8; '*my gentle love*', l. 232; '*sweeting*', l. 234; Desdemona: '*dear*', l. 233. Othello has not been intimate with her before the wedding nor does she give any signs of having been abused or coerced as her father suggested. Their wedding night is interrupted by the 'ruckus' in the guards' room, but there is no sign of this casting a shadow over their bliss.

When Iago begins insinuating that Desdemona is unfaithful, Othello holds back his misgivings and hides his suspicions. He sends his wife away and rejects her help when Desdemona wants to nurse his feigned headache, though she is sorry that he feels unwell. From then on, goaded by Iago's vivid descriptions of adultery and false accusations, Othello gradually loses his self-control and finally turns into a wife-killer.

From the start, Iago's and Emilia's relationship seems rather love-less. He is disrespectful and sarcastic towards her in public (II, 1) and privately (*'foolish wife'*, III, iii, l. 305) and includes her in his diatribe about women. Iago cannot trust or love anyone but is not immune to sexual jealousy when he suspects her of having been unfaithful with Othello and Cassio. Emilia stoically receives his insults, remains eager to please him, though, and shows him the handkerchief he wanted her to steal. Iago is dismissive towards her and snatches the handkerchief out of her hand, but he also praises her for stealing it. He does not in-clude her in his plans and thus makes her an unwitting accomplice. Between these two, little romance or display of love is found. Emilia is more loyal to Iago than to Desdemona until she finds out about his intrigues, when she reveals Iago's actions and is stabbed by him in re-prisal.

Cassio and Bianca's relationship seems like a tawdry affair, typical of a soldier who is accustomed to finding women wherever he is sta-tioned. Though repeatedly insulted as a whore, Bianca does not appear to be one and truly loves Cassio, which becomes apparent when she sees him wounded.

Iago and Emilia's relationship as well as Cassio and Bianca's echo the main plot of Othello and Desdemona's marriage in that they also deal with a lack of trust and jealousy, but they are never developed into a sub-plot so as not to divert from the tragic main action.

▶▶▶ Themes

Jealousy

In psychology, the phenomenon of excessive sexual jealousy is called 'Othello Syndrome', after Shakespeare's well-known tragic hero who displays this overriding feeling or flaw of character so impressively. Other characters experience jealousy as well, though not in such an existential way. Initially claiming that he is not jealous (III, iii, ll. 177–193), Othello soon succumbs to overwhelming jealousy. He has epileptic fits, looks shaken to the core and cannot even speak in his calm, measured manner anymore. Forgetting all rational thinking, Othello does not seek to find out if Iago's allegations are true but takes circumstantial evidence and hearsay for the truth. There was little time and opportunity for Desdemona and her supposed lover Cassio to have met and have had illicit relations, because she was either in her father's or Othello's care, and Cassio sailed to Cyprus on a separate ship. Othello sees Emilia's protestations of Desdemona's fidelity as women's complicity and has adopted Iago's misogynistic views completely. He trusts his fellow soldier more than his wife and cannot bear the idea of being a cuckold ('*A hornèd man's a monster and a beast.*', IV, i, l. 60).

Iago mentions that he feels sexual jealousy for Othello and Cassio (I, iii, ll. 366–368; II, i, ll. 275–284; II, i, ll. 288), whom he both suspects of having slept with his wife Emilia, but he does not act on it by accusing them or finding proof of their guilt. Instead, he involves both men in his scheme of vengeance. Being a good judge of character, Iago assesses the workings of jealousy on Othello quite well: '*Trifles light as air are to the jealous confirmations strong as proofs of holy writ: this may do something.*' (III, iii, ll. 322–324).

Two minor characters, Roderigo and Bianca, Cassio's mistress, complain about other characters of whom they are jealous. Roderigo is a jilted lover whose hopes of finally winning Desdemona for himself are kindled by Iago, and he expresses his hopeless love for Desdemona graphically (I, iii, ll. 301–305; 311–312). Bianca's brief appearance characterises her as deeply in love with Cassio, who does not reciprocate her feelings and has no qualms to enjoy her favours in private while ridiculing her in public. Bianca suspects Cassio of having another lover when he hands her the handkerchief he found and seems to be the only one who might have grounds for being jealous, since Cassio's behaviour towards women is flirtatious (IV, i, ll. 141–147).

Iago's plotting was set in motion by his professional and probably justified jealousy of Cassio, whose promotion to lieutenant seems to be based rather on political or private reasons than on merit or military experience. '*Preferment goes by letter and affection, and not by old gradation, where each second stood heir to the first.*' (I, i, ll. 36–38).

Emilia is the only one who identifies Othello's erratic behaviour correctly as driven by jealousy, while Desdemona naively thinks that, because she has not done anything to deserve such suspicion, her husband cannot be jealous (III, iv, ll. 149–156).

Since Shakespeare explores this theme on so many levels and with so many characters, one of which is even killed in spite of her innocence, it can safely be called the main theme of the play.

Male honour and female chastity

In Shakespeare's time, people followed a set of beliefs now called the 'Elizabethan World View' (cf. 'Life in Renaissance England', p. 7). It was based on the Bible and contained a strict hierarchical system with God in heaven at the top, the king on earth below him and humans, animals and plants in succession according to their supposed worth. In this concept, women were seen as inferior to men and had to obey their fathers or husbands who regarded them as their possessions. If a woman behaved disrespectfully, she brought shame on her male protector's head and had to be punished. The worst sin a wife could commit was to have sex with another man and thus make her husband a cuckold, who became a common laughing stock and whose honour was then compromised.

In *Othello*, all men display little trust in the women's loyalty and faithfulness and speak in derogatory ways about them, although they have little reason to do so, because none of them behaves improperly. Desdemona and Emilia discuss sexual behaviour in marriage when Emilia believes Othello to be jealous. She speaks out in favour of equal treatment and mutual respect of both sexes for each other and suggests that women 'stray' only because their husbands set such examples. Whereas Desdemona categorically rejects unfaithfulness, Emilia could imagine it to further Iago's career, which sheds a light on the different marital affection they feel (IV, iii, ll. 62–99).

Shakespeare shows the women's true natures and depicts Desdemona as the innocent victim of Iago's slander. Othello's inflated sense of self and his hurt pride make him kill Desdemona without any proof to maintain his male honour which he sees in question. He regains some of his former stature when he realises his error in regard to Iago's comprehensive deception and commits suicide.

Brabantio feels that, after Desdemona's flight and marriage, his social standing is at stake, which is a mésalliance in his eyes and '*incur[s] a general mock*' (I, ii, l. 69). In act V, his brother Gratiano informs the other characters that Brabantio died of grief after having been so dishonoured in Venice.

As the main male characters are soldiers and conscious of their social and military positions, their professional honour is at stake as well, particularly for Iago, who feels slighted and overlooked for promotion (I, i, ll. 8–33).

Being the mastermind that he is, Iago pulls all the strings to trigger the other men's self-esteem and achieve the expected reactions. He invites men '*that hold their honours in a wary distance*' (II, iii, l. 48) to celebrate with Cassio, which turns into a general brawl. When Cassio bemoans his loss of reputation at length after having been demoted for unsuitable behaviour in the line of duty ('*I have lost the immortal part of my soul*', II, iii, l. 244), Iago comforts him with: '*Reputation is an idle and most false imposition*' (II, iii, l. 248). To convince Othello of what he wants him to believe, he claims the complete opposite, namely that a stained reputation will dishonour both sexes: '*Good name in man and woman [...] is the immediate jewel of their souls [...].*' (III, iii, ll. 156–157).

Othello's social inferiority as a black man in Venice's rich and white aristocratic society, despite his professional achievements as an army general, adds to his insecurities about his honour and societal esteem.

Performance History and Criticism

During Shakespeare's lifetime, three performances of *Othello* are recorded, the first for King James I in 1604, and documents state that the other two were presented at the Globe Theatre and in Oxford in 1610. Till 1636, more court performances followed until all theatres were permanently closed in 1642. After the Civil War and Charles II's coronation (his father Charles I had been executed) the theatres reopened in 1660. The king allowed actresses to perform, and it is generally believed that the first woman to act on an English stage played the role of Desdemona. The famous diarist and avid theatre-goer Samuel Pepys went to see a production in the same year and noted the shock at Desdemona's death among the audience.

During the Restoration period in the 18th century, *Othello* was regularly put on stage, but troubling scenes like Othello's fit and his striking Desdemona were cut to suit the taste of the times. Throughout the following centuries, renowned actors and actresses of their time, such as David Garrick, Edmund Kean, Henry Irving, Ellen Terry and Sarah Siddons, took the key roles, which impressed their audiences greatly according to contemporary theatre reviews. Like the best actors of our time, they were drawn to these parts because the characters' inner selves must be convincingly revealed in order to make their feelings and emotional development plausible. There are few action-filled scenes in *Othello*, and no sub-plot diverts the viewers' attention, which is concentrated on the human drama of a few protagonists.

In the 19th century, there were two black American actors on British stages, who had fled from the US segregation laws, Ira Aldridge and James Hewlett. Aldridge's first appearance as Othello caused an uproar, and the production had to be cancelled. Due to racist attitudes that prevailed at the time, the spectators could not tolerate seeing a black man touching a white woman. Another critic, Charles Lamb, with the prejudices of his times, pointed out that the experience of reading the play was quite different to seeing it in that one feels more moved by Othello's noble character and his distress on the page than on stage, where his 'otherness' is so visible.

In the 20th century, the British acting legend Laurence Olivier played Othello in a National Theatre production in 1964. It was captured on film and was seen as a 'definitive' performance that could not be rivalled for a long time. The lead was also performed by Orson Welles (in a film version in 1952), on stage by Anthony Hopkins (1981) and Ben Kingsley (1985), and by Laurence Fishburne in another film version in 1995. Iago's role was played by prominent actors like Ian McKellen, David Suchet and Bob Hoskins.

Up to the 1980s, Othello was played by white actors in 'blackface', i.e. with black make-up. This is no longer done due to present-day notions of political correctness. However, some black actors have expressed concern about playing the role. According to them, personifying a black man in a discrediting presentation in an otherwise white cast will reinforce existing prejudices. To counteract this, director Iqbal Khan had an ethnically mixed ensemble in his 2015 production, with Iago being black as well. The famous (white) actor and director Steven Berkoff thinks that letting only black actors play Othello is 'racism in reverse'. In the 20th century, prominent African-American actors, such as Paul Robeson or James Earl Jones, have played the part, which Robeson even called his 'life role'.

In recent years, there have been several noteworthy productions of *Othello* by the National Theatre (2013), the Royal Shakespeare Company (2015) and the Donmar Warehouse Theatre (2007). Their theatrical trailers give an adequate impression of the impact the play can have on the viewers. The production of Shakespeare's Globe Theatre (2007) can be viewed online on the theatre's *Video on Demand* platform, and a new production premiered in July 2018. In their advertisement, they have used the pun of separating the syllable 'hell' in 'Othello' in a different colour.

Some directors, who disapprove of the text, have challenged the established interpretation of the play. In Trevor Nunn's production of 1990 for instance, Desdemona tries (in vain) to escape from the room. Charles Marowitz' production called *An Othello* (1972) had a black Iago destroy Othello because he has betrayed his fellow blacks by trying to be part of the white society. Using additional scenes, the director made Desdemona a whore who was enjoyed by the 'general camp' of soldiers. Lodovico cut Othello's throat when he hesitated to kill himself, whereupon Desdemona (not dead) rose from her bed.

Most directors today, however, merely cut the text and add stage business to demonstrate their take on the play, but do not deconstruct or alter it completely in order to show their disagreement with the message of the play, as it is done on many European stages.

Up to the 20th century, traditional criticism of *Othello* has adopted the Aristotelian definition of a tragic hero whose fate is inescapable. Critics of this school have concentrated on the study of the characters and treated them as if they were real human beings. They considered the hero afflicted with a tragic flaw, in this case Othello's jealousy, which mainly caused the tragedy. By some, Othello was described as wooden and lacking in insight and depth while others praised his honesty. Harold Bloom (*Shakespeare: The Invention of the Human* (1998)) considers *Othello* Shakespeare's most offensive representation of male arrogance and demonisation of female sexuality. Other critics have suggested that Desdemona is partly to blame for her fate, because she lied about the handkerchief and could have averted some of the ensuing complications. Another view is that the persistent way in which she nags Othello about forgiving Cassio seems out of order for someone who does not have any personal interest. This 'character criticism' does not include any social, economic, historical or political factors which are dealt with in modern critical approaches.

In the first half of the 20th century, different critics saw Shakespeare's plays as explorations of important themes (e.g. the conflict between appearance and reality), as they have image-clusters as a dominant feature (e.g. black/evil vs. white/good imagery) or thought the plays should be studied for their poetic language or their stagecraft.

Critical approaches to Shakespeare's plays were radically transformed in the last quarter of the 20th century, when 'modern criticism' focused on singular viewpoints, often opposed to each other.

Political criticism sees the characters as determined by the historical conditions of the time and the society they lived in. Viewed from this standpoint, Iago would be both the victim and the enforcer of a corrupt society and Othello the outcast who was employed when needed, but not good enough to join Venice's aristocratic circles.

Influenced by Sigmund Freud's theories, psychological criticism refers to the characters' unconscious and irrational desires, fears and sexuality. This approach suggests that there is a 'hidden content' behind the 'manifest content' of the text or play itself, which, however, cannot be proved. Therefore, Iago's motivations for his plotting are of interest. His references to sexual behaviour have led to an interest in Iago's own sexual nature, and a repressed homo-erotic desire has been suggested. At the end of III, 3, when he takes vows with Othello, this moment has been interpreted as a version of the marriage vow, especially as he says, '*I am your own forever*' in reply to Othello's '*Now art thou my lieutenant*' (ll. 480; 479). Being the spin-doctor that he is, this could also be Iago's subterfuge to betray Othello, like Iago's invented sexual dream Cassio supposedly had of Desdemona.

Feminist criticism or gender studies challenge sexism and point out how female experience is shown or how pervasive the patriarchal ideas are. Men define their honour by the chastity of their wives and dread any hint of cuckoldry. The male characters have a warped view of women and their sexuality, loyalty and truthfulness, which is put into perspective by the way Shakespeare shows the female characters' true natures. All the same, the men very often portray women in demeaning ways and see them as whores.

Feminist critics would argue that Desdemona, Emilia and Bianca together shape the plot, the conflict and the themes of the play while the men are so obsessed with male honour that tragedy follows. The women would be criticised for giving too much priority to their partner instead of recognising what they have in common with each other. Emilia's speech on the equality of men and women in marriage is thus regarded as an expression of early feminist thinking. The fact that Shakespeare has her say these lines shows that he must have seen women as equal in a world where they were not.

In recent years, *Othello* has come under close scrutiny because the play has been suspected of propagating racism. Directors of modern productions often make a point of addressing this issue in theatre programmes, in online videos or in discussions after the performances. Critics who think *Othello* is racist argue that several characters are bigoted towards Othello and use racial slurs (Iago, Brabantio, Roderigo) and that he is not welcome in Brabantio's family. Also, when he is shown in his jealous fury, his character traits derive from typically crude racist views (lustful, violent temper, barbarous).

People taking a contrary stance argue that the play examines racism, but does not propagate it and that we focus on the question of race because it is politically correct to do so in our time. Other characters in the play, such as the Duke of Venice himself or Desdemona, are characters who clearly oppose the racist attitudes of others. A further argument is that if racism had been meant to be a focal issue, it would have taken up much more room. On the other hand, staging *Othello* in countries with official segregation has served as a political issue to criticise the government and as a symbol in the fight for emancipation. The director Janet Suzman and her ensemble saw their production of *Othello* in South Africa in 1987 as a statement against apartheid. The male lead, black actor John Kani, said he identified with Othello through his experience as a black South African, because he felt like an alien in his own country. At the time, interracial marriages were forbidden, and outraged members of the audience left the theatre when Othello and Desdemona kissed in II, 1.

▶▶▶ Language, Style and Dramatic Devices

The differences in the language of Othello and Iago

Most of Iago and Othello's key scenes are notable for their great verse language. Shakespeare makes the contrast between the two characters evident in the way they speak. Othello's verses change from dignified, poetic, even heroic language reflecting his authority to near inarticulateness with broken syntax, clipped exclamations and oaths. Under Iago's spell, Othello adopts the latter's way of speaking, too, until he returns to his former speech when his jealous rage is spent and he faces his own death at the end. Iago mostly uses prose with simple vocabulary in a neutral register when speaking publicly, but is far more eloquent in his soliloquies. He can adapt his speech to the person he addresses and often uses the blunt orders of a soldier. The beauty of Othello's way of speaking has been called 'Othello Music' by critics. His rhetorical skills, which give him such persuasive power over Othello, are Iago's strong point.

Othello's language

In the first act set in Venice, Othello's speeches are in keeping with the social environment he finds himself in – he pays his respects to the duke and the senators and addresses them in a high-flown style: '*Most potent, grave, and reverend signiors, my very noble and approved good masters [...].*' (I, iii, ll. 76–77). In the previous scene, when Brabantio and his men confront him and his soldiers, Othello remains unperturbed and manages to calm the angry crowd with just a few sentences: '*Keep up (= put down) your bright swords, for the dew will rust them.*' (I, ii, l. 59) and '*Hold your hands, both you of my inclining, and the rest: Were it my cue to fight, I should have known it without a prompter.*' (I, ii, ll. 81–84). Before recounting the story of his life, Othello claims to be '*rude*' (l. 81) in his speech and '*little blessed with the soft phrase of peace*' (I, iii, l. 82), which is false modesty. He has not only held Desdemona and her father spellbound, who loved to listen to his tales, but prompts the duke to say that '*this tale would win [his] daughter too*' (I, iii, l. 170). In Cyprus, before Iago has begun his devious corruption, Othello expresses his joy of being reunited with Desdemona. He compares his powerful emotions with natural elements that have no bounds, like the sky, the wind and the sea or with boundless entities like heaven, hell, fate or death (II, i, ll. 178–186). His love for Desdemona also manifests itself in the many terms of endearment he uses in II, 1 (*'o my fair warrior!'*, l. 175; *'O my soul's joy!'*, l. 177; *'Honey'*, l. 197; *'o my sweet'*, l. 198) and II, 3 (*'my dear love'*, l. 8; *'my gentle love'*, l. 232; *'sweeting'*, l. 234).

As soon as suspicion has taken root in Othello's mind, he experiences conflicting emotions. It is a theatrical convention to make characters speak the truth in a soliloquy. In his monologue in III, 3, Othello is not completely sure whether Desdemona is dishonest or not (III, iii, ll. 261–264). He will throw her out if this is so and hate her for putting him, the *'great one[..]'* (l. 274), into the position of a cuckold (III, iii, ll. 274–278). Othello searches for reasons for her unfaithfulness and broods on his own imagined deficiencies, using imagery: *'I am declined into the vale of years'*, (III, iii, ll. 266–267). He feels slighted in his manhood and honour and generally blames women for their fickleness (III, iii, ll. 269–271). Othello's comparisons here refer to disgusting images of nature: *'I had rather be a toad and live upon the vapour of a dungeon than keep a corner in the thing I love for others' uses.'* (III, iii, ll. 271–274). Later in the scene, he feels he has even lost his military career and all the pomp and trappings of warfare: *'Farewell the plumèd troops [...] Othello's occupation's gone!'* (III, iii, ll. 350–358). Desdemona is now described as a *'fair devil'* (III, iii, l. 479), who is blackened by sin and he compares her to his own skin colour: *'Her name, that was as fresh as Dian's visage, is now begrimed and black as mine own face.'* (III, iii, ll. 387–389).

Othello's determination to kill his wife is revealed in drastic terms: *'I'll tear her all to pieces.'* (III, iii, l. 432); *'I will chop her into messes (= pieces): cuckold me!'* (IV, i, l. 186). At the end of III, 3, Othello resorts to imagery that includes references to heaven and hell (III, iii, ll. 446–451) or to unstoppable water currents (III, iii, ll. 454–461). Again, this underlines his strong feelings, save that they have now turned against Desdemona, whom he wants to punish: *'Damn her, lewd minx! O, damn her!'* (III, iii, l. 476). He kneels down as if for a prayer and vows to kill her: *'In the due reverence of a sacred vow I here engage my words.'* (III, iii, ll. 462-463), which is blasphemous, since God's commandments explicitly forbid murder.

Othello's language is now marked by more sentence fragments, exclamations and repetitions, which reveals his agitation. His way of speaking forms an obvious contrast to his measured speech in earlier scenes.

In act IV, when Iago has plagued him with graphic images of Desdemona sleeping with Cassio, he can only babble before he loses consciousness: *'Lie with her! Lie on her! [...] Pish! Noses, ears and lips. Is't possible – Confess? Handkerchief! O devil!'* (IV, i, ll. 35–41). When Othello talks directly with Desdemona, his language deteriorates even more. It is now often characterised by a lack of fluency, and he mainly uses questions, orders and insults (*'impudent strumpet'*, *'cunning whore'*, IV, ii, ll. 80; 88).

In his longer passages, where he describes his resentment to Desdemona's alleged infidelity, Othello employs imagery which is mainly taken from nature and the cosmos but also from business in brothels.

The literary device of antithesis is used in Othello's references to heaven and hell: *'being like one of heaven, the devils themselves should fear to seize thee'* (IV, ii, ll. 35–36); *'Heaven truly knows thou art false as hell.'* (IV, ii, l. 38); *'where either I must live, or bear no life'* (IV, ii, l. 57); *'the fountain from the which my current runs, or else dries up'* (IV, ii, ll. 58–59); *'You, mistress (Emilia), that have the office opposite to Saint Peter (= heaven), and keep the gate of hell!'* (IV, ii, ll. 89–91).

Images of beauty and purity are directly contrasted with references to hell, death or sin: *'Patience, thou young and rose-lipped cherubin; ay, there, look grim as hell!'* (IV, ii, ll. 62–63); *'O thou weed, who art so lovely fair and smell'st so sweet that the sense aches at thee, would thou hadst ne'er been born!'* (IV, ii, ll. 66–68); *'Was this fair paper, this most goodly book, made to write 'whore' upon?'* (IV, ii, ll. 70–71).

Heaven, the moon and the wind are personified and given human traits. They shut off their senses to avoid being confronted with Desdemona's sin: *'Heaven stops the nose at it and the moon winks, the bawdy wind that kisses all it meets is hushed within the hollow mine of earth, and will not hear it.'* (IV, ii, ll. 76–79).

Othello's mounting fury is shown by his repetition of disbelief *'(What) committed!'* (4x), when his wife has asked him *'Alas, what ignorant sin have I committed?'* (IV, ii, ll. 69 ff.).

Othello contrasts his deliberate exaggeration of Desdemona's guilt with the hyperbolic description of his own virtue: '*Had it pleased heaven to try me with affliction; had they rained all kinds of sores and shames on my bare head, steeped me in poverty to the very lips, given to captivity me and my utmost hopes, I should have found in some place of my soul a drop of patience.*' (IV, ii, ll. 46–52); '*I should make very forges of my cheeks, that would to cinders burn up modesty, did I but speak thy deeds.*' (IV, ii, ll. 73–75).

Images from nature describing reproduction in dark, dank or decaying places are used to convey disgust at Desdemona's supposed lovemaking, such as '*toads*' in '*cisterns*' (IV, ii, ll. 60–61) or '*flies*' in slaughter-houses (IV, ii, l. 65).

To show his disgust, Othello repeatedly compares Emilia to a madam and his wife to a prostitute working in a brothel: Emilia is called a '*simple bawd*', '*subtle whore*' (IV, ii, ll. 19; 20) who provides services to customers: '*a closet lock and key of villainous secrets*'; '*Some of your function, mistress; leave procreants alone and shut the door; cough, or cry 'hem', if anybody come [...].*'; '*We have done our course; there's money for your pains. I pray you, turn the key and keep our counsel.*' (IV, ii, ll. 21; 26–28; 92–93).

Othello calls Desdemona a '*whore*' (IV, ii, ll. 71; 85), '*public commoner*' (IV, ii, l. 72), '*(impudent) strumpet*' (IV, ii, ll. 80; 81) and, using irony, '*I cry you mercy, then: I took you for that cunning whore of Venice that married with Othello.*' (IV, ii, ll. 87–89). He cannot even hide his discomposure in the company of the Venetian visitors, who are quite stupefied to observe Othello's transformation (IV, i, ll. 240–251).

In V, 2, Othello once more undergoes a fundamental change in regard to his feelings for Desdemona: he turns from a ruthless killer into a man desperate enough to find death by his own hand when he has become aware of her innocence. In ll. 1–22, when he is looking at his sleeping wife, Othello repeats some phrases several times, which almost gives an impression of musicality ('*it is the cause*', '*put out the light*', '*one more [kiss]*'). He admires Desdemona's beauty and uses imagery to compare her to marble statues, light he will extinguish or a rose he will pluck. These poetic expressions form a striking contrast to what he intends to do. When he looks at her lifeless body, Othello's imagery describes all-encompassing darkness, a world that is out of joint: '*Methinks it should be now a huge eclipse of sun and moon, and that the affrighted globe should yawn at alteration.*' (V, ii, ll. 99–101).

This state of things is anticipated in his remark in III, 3, when he says, '*Perdition catch my soul, but I do love thee! And when I love thee not, chaos is come again.*' (III, iii, ll. 90–92). During the course of the play and thinking himself justified, Othello has given the term 'justice' a new definition by his and Iago's perversion of its concept.

After having realised Iago's colossal deception, Othello concedes Desdemona's innocence and employs cosmic imagery in V, 2, ll. 270–279. Just her glance at him in heaven will throw him down to hell expecting his deserved punishment, which is described using hyperbole and exclamations ('*whip me...*', '*blow me...*', '*roast me...*', '*wash me...*'). A howl of grief ends his anguish: '*O Desdemona! Desdemona! Dead! O! O! O!*' (V, ii, l. 279).

In his final speech, before he kills himself, Othello reverts to the measured, regular verse he used at the beginning of the play. Almost as if it were an obituary, he looks back at his life and achievements, regrets his deed and finds some excuse for his wife's murder that not all characters present might share: '*one that loved not wisely, but too well*' (V, ii, l. 340). His loyalty to the Venetian state seems important to him as he mentions it twice and his last words refer to a '*turbaned Turk*' (V, ii, l. 349) he killed who spoke ill of Venice. His own sorrow finds its expression in imagery relating to a '*base Indian*' (V, ii, l. 343) who does not know the value of a precious '*pearl*' and throws it away. '*Trees*' bleeding liquid in great quantities, like Othello sheds tears of anguish (V, ii, ll. 341–347) is another metaphor expressing this.

Iago's rhetorical skills

Shakespeare uses soliloquies or asides to show how Iago's mind works. This way, he can divulge his aims and motives when he is alone on stage, because he cannot let anyone in on his secrets. Due to this theatrical device, the audience is informed of his plotting from the start, otherwise they would not understand what is going on and be as clueless as Iago's victims. Their involuntary complicity adds to the suspense the viewers feel who always know more than the characters on stage.

Iago mostly speaks in prose, often using the crude language of a soldier with drastic descriptions, such as his animal imagery when referring to the couple's '*unnatural*' (III, iii, ll. 230–234) intercourse that will result in horse-like offspring (I, i, ll. 89–90; 111–113; 115–116). His demeaning comments on other characters show his cynicism towards everyone: he calls Othello an '*ass[..]*' (I, iii, l. 382), his wife '*foolish*' (III, iii, l. 305), Roderigo '*poor trash*' (II, i, l. 284), just to give some examples. His prediction in terms of Othello and Desdemona's change in behaviour proves his disdain of genuine emotions ('*It cannot be that Desdemona should long continue her love to the Moor [...].*', '*Moors are changeable*', I, iii, ll. 332–333; 335–336). When he scoffs at Roderigo's lovesickness, he calls women '*guinea-hen[s] (= prostitutes)*' (I, iii, l. 309) and reacts to the word '*virtue*' with an obscene gesture ('*a fig*', I, iii, ll. 313; 313). Although the Venetian gentleman Roderigo is his social superior, Iago lectures him and uses imperatives to manipulate him (e.g. I, i, ll. 68–74). Roderigo himself speaks in prose, which is normally reserved for lowly characters or villains.

Iago's ability to manipulate others through language can be explained by his superior mastery of rhetoric and figurative language. He is a keen observer who reads body language correctly and skilfully applies his knowledge to his ends. In I, 2, Iago exhibits his duplicitous techniques, when he claims Roderigo slandered Othello, and Iago pretends he wanted to fight with him in order to ingratiate himself with Othello (I, ii, ll. 1–10). In the 'Temptation scene' (III, 3), the audience is given ample time to watch Iago trick Othello into believing that Desdemona is unfaithful. He arouses suspicion when Cassio ends his talk with Desdemona quickly and leaves, saying '*Ha! I like not that.*' (l. 35) and '*Cassio, my lord! No, sure, I cannot think it, that he would steal away so guilty-like, seeing you coming.*' (ll. 38–40). Asking leading questions ('*Did Michael Cassio [...] know of your love?*', ll. 93–94) and meaningfully repeating Othello's words in short questions or exclamations, he casts doubt on Cassio ('*Indeed!*', l. 100; '*Honest, my lord!*', l. 103; '*Think, my lord!*', l. 107).

Iago uses these repetitions as well to create well-placed moments of silence or hesitation that slyly hint at things he seemingly does not want to speak about. This tactic spurs people on to imagine a worst-case scenario. His praise of Cassio is insincere ('*I dare be sworn I think that he is honest.*', l. 126), and his comment on Othello calling Desdemona honest suggests the opposite ('*And long live you to think so!*', l. 227). When Othello gets more and more upset, Iago directly comments on his state of mind to add to the impact of his words: '*I see this hath a little dashed your spirits.*'; '*My lord, I see you're moved.*' (ll. 215; 225). Othello denies this, but his short answers prove he is preoccupied with Iago's lies. When Othello's vulnerability becomes more evident, Iago hypocritically advises him not to take the matter too seriously (ll. 245–256) and have trust in both his wife and Cassio. He even pretends wounded innocence and surprise when Othello begins to rail at Desdemona and bemoans his hurt pride, feigning remorse for what he said to Othello (ll. 374–381). A moment of doubt that Desdemona could really be disloyal is shown when Othello asks for '*ocular proof*' (l. 361) of Iago's allegations. Using sexual imagery to wound Othello, Iago muses that it will be difficult to catch the adulterers in the act: '*Would you, the supervisor (= onlooker), grossly gape on – behold her topped?*' (ll. 396–397). He mentions animals supposed to be lustful in Elizabethan times to underline the bestial act ('*as prime as goats, as hot as monkeys, as salt as wolves in pride*', ll. 404–405) before he offers his circumstantial evidence which consists of downright lies. It is the inflammatory imagery of Cassio speaking of Desdemona in his sleep or wiping his beard with the handkerchief that has Othello on the brink of collapse. Having reached his aim, Iago again recommends patience and lenience ('*your mind perhaps may change*'; '*But let her live.*' ll. 453; 475), while simultaneously vowing to help the '*wronged Othello[..]*' (l. 468) in '*what bloody business ever*' (l. 470). He mimics Othello's earnestness and kneels down with him, swearing the false oath that he will be '*[Othello's] own forever*' (l. 480).

Up to this point, Iago has succeeded in creating three false identities: that Cassio is a reckless drunkard, Desdemona a whore and he himself a perfectly honest and trustworthy man.

In act IV, Iago continues his tactic to inflame Othello's jealousy with leading questions that call Desdemona's honour and behaviour towards men into question: '*To kiss in private?*'; '*Or to be naked with her friend in bed an hour or more, not meaning any harm?*'; '*Her honour is an essence that's not seen; they have it very oft that have it not [...]*', IV, i, ll. 2; 3–4; 16–17). Wanting to incite Othello's fury, Iago deliberately hesitates before he tells him that Cassio boasts of having slept with Desdemona (IV, i, ll. 23–34), which brings about Othello's fit of epilepsy. Gloating over his success, Iago says, '*Work on, my medicine, work! Thus credulous fools are caught; and many worthy and chaste dames even thus, all guiltless, meet reproach.'* (IV, i, ll. 42–45). Othello agrees to listen to the conversation Iago will have with Cassio, for which Iago prepares Othello in order to achieve a conditioned response. Iago tells him to watch Cassio's body language, which supposedly refers to his intimate encounters with Desdemona. However, Iago intends to speak with him about Bianca and counts on his behaviour to make it seem as if Cassio spoke about Desdemona (IV, i, ll. 79–85; 91–101). Thinking on his feet, Iago uses Bianca's appearance and her giving Cassio the handkerchief back to strengthen Othello's conviction of Desdemona's foul play with his lieutenant.

When the Venetian visitor Lodovico asks how Cassio is, Iago answers ironically: *'Lives, sir.'* (IV, i, l. 209). In their conversation, Iago shows his cleverness by suggesting an opinion without actually expressing it, namely that Othello's mind is sick. He feigns concern and loyalty to his superior officer and advises Lodovico to draw his own conclusions (IV, i, ll. 252–269), even though Lodovico has already remarked on how unhinged Othello's mind is.

Iago's plans do not fully come to fruition in V, 1, when Roderigo's attack on Cassio fails and Iago has to step in, stabbing Cassio in the leg. It is dark in the street when Lodovico and Gratiano appear and recognise Iago who must pretend to help Cassio although he would have liked to get rid of his enemy there and then. Iago claims he has arrived only recently and kills Roderigo, unseen. His next tactic to deflect the others' attention from why he is there at all is to blame Bianca and accuse her of being involved in the street fight. He realises that his plotting might not have the desired effect now that Cassio has survived the assault on him: *'This is the night that either makes me or fordoes (= ruins) me quite.'* (V, i, ll. 128–129).

Due to Emilia's exposure of Iago's intrigues in V, 2, he finds himself on the defensive and he only replies in short sentences, not admitting anything: *'I told him what I thought, and told no more than what he found himself was apt and true.'* (V, ii, ll. 174–175). Trying several times to hush his wife and order her home before his guilt is fully revealed, Iago loses his composure and insults her, denying her reproach: *'Villainous whore!'*; *'Filth, thou liest!'* (V, ii, ll. 226; 228). In retaliation, he stabs her and runs away, but is caught and brought back as a prisoner.

In a last act of spite, Iago refuses to give reasons why he deceived Othello and plotted Cassio's death: '*Demand me nothing: what you know, you know: from this time forth I never will speak word.*' (V, ii, ll. 300–301). Thus, the tragic hero Othello has the final word in the play and not the villain who engineered his downfall.

Imagery and Symbols

Apart from Othello's **imagery** referring to nature and the cosmos and Iago's metaphorical language describing animals mentioned before, the opposition between 'white/fair/angel' versus 'black/dark/devil' is presented on many levels. Traditionally, the colour 'white' has been associated with goodness, purity and virtue, whereas the colour 'black' is stereotypically connected to evil, corruption and deceit.

The interracial marriage of a black man to a white woman is at the heart of the play, and Othello is the only black character in Venice and Cyprus' white society. This visual contrast portrayed by the actors has its impact on the audience throughout the performance. The setting of the play shifts from 'night in Venice' to 'daylight in Cyprus', and additional scenes in which evil acts are committed, such as the drinking scene, the street fight and Desdemona's murder, all take place at night. Iago's evil plans are often devised in the dark of night, when he is alone.

Many times, the contrast between black and white is used in the same sentence to heighten the effect of the images (antithesis), e.g. in Iago's sneer: '*an old black ram is tupping your white ewe*' (I, i, ll. 89–90) or the duke's remark to Brabantio: '*Your son-in-law is far more fair than black*' (I, iii, l. 286). 'Fair' also meant 'good', 'virtuous' and 'blond', while 'black' could refer to brunette hair as well. The references to hair colour are made use of when Desdemona and Iago are bantering while waiting for Othello's ship to land. They discuss women who are '*fair and wise*', '*black and witty*' and '*fair and foolish*' (II, i, ll. 129–134).

Iago's intention is to turn Desdemona's '*virtue into pitch (= black tar)*' (II, iii, l. 331), which is echoed by Othello when he is convinced of her impurity: '*Her name, that was as fresh as Dian's visage, is now be-grimed and black as mine own face*' (III, iii, ll. 387–389). After having killed his wife, Othello says of Desdemona: '*She's, like a liar, gone to burning hell: 'twas I that killed her.*' (V, ii, ll. 129–130). Emilia angrily retorts: '*O, the more angel she, and you the blacker devil!*' (V, ii, ll. 130–131).

Desdemona herself consistently uses religious imagery and often refers to 'heaven', 'soul' and 'God'. In front of the senate, she '*consecrates*' her '*soul and fortunes*' to Othello (I, iii, l. 250). Witnessing the change in Othello, she prays: '*O, heaven forgive us!*', '*by this light of heaven*' and '*here I kneel*' (IV, ii, ll. 87; 149; 150). On her deathbed, she pleads: '*Then heaven have mercy on me!*' (V, ii, ll. 33–34) and '*Then Lord have mercy on me!*' (V, ii, l. 57).

Suspected witchcraft or 'black' magic is depicted in other imagery used in the play. Brabantio furiously confronts Othello with: '*Damned as thou art, thou hast enchanted her; for I'll refer me to all things of sense, if she in chains of magic were not bound*' (I, ii, ll. 63–65). In the council chamber in front of the senators, he accuses Othello again, unable to imagine his daughter might have gone with him voluntarily: '*She is abused and stol'n from me, and corrupted by spells and medicines bought of mountebanks; for nature so preposterously to err, being not deficient, blind or lame of sense, sans witchcraft could not.*' (I, iii, ll. 60–64). He repeats his firm belief that '*practices of cunning hell*' and '*mixtures powerful o'er the blood*' (I, iii, ll. 102; 104) must have been administered.

When Othello recounts the story of how the handkerchief came to possess magical powers in III, 4, it is supposed to be more beneficial, maybe like 'white' magic: An Egyptian sorceress or witch put a spell on it so that the person sharing it would be loved by the recipient. This charm worked on Othello's father, and his mother gave it to her son to pass it on to his future wife. If it were lost, this would end in a catastrophe, however (III, iv, ll. 51–64). The silk worms producing the threads for the cloth were '*hallowed (= holy)*' and a fortune-teller, who was 200 years old, sewed the handkerchief which was then dyed in a liquid people produced using mummified hearts of virgins (III, iv, ll. 65–71).

In this play, the main **symbols** are all interconnected and add to the inevitable tragic ending. Sorrow to come is anticipated by the *Willow Song* (IV, 3), the handkerchief is the trigger for the murder, and finally the marital bed also serves as the resting place for the dead couple. Together they all underline the intended effect.

The handkerchief as a prop is also an example of how stage objects can be invested with meaning through the power of suggestion.

Dramatic structure

There are very few *stage directions* in Shakespeare's plays. Mostly, he indicates what the actors are supposed to do in their lines, e.g. when Desdemona says, '*here I kneel*' (IV, ii, l. 150) or, to Othello, '*Alas, why gnaw you so your nether lip?*' (V, ii, l. 43).

Othello is a little unusual concerning its *structure*. Generally, the *inciting action*, or what sets the plot in motion, happens in the initial scenes of the first act. Here, the action already happened before the play starts – it is the marriage of Othello and Desdemona. Iago and Roderigo enter discussing their elopement and inform Desdemona's father Brabantio of her flight. What follows in the three scenes of the first act is the confrontation between Brabantio and Othello, which is resolved when Othello and Desdemona explain their courtship and marriage in front of the duke. Iago's plan to destroy the couple's union and to revenge himself for not being promoted advances the action.

Shakespeare scholars have not agreed on where the *climax* and the *falling action* of the play are placed.

Some scholars find the moment in III, 3, when Othello swears to kill his wife, climactic, since it describes the typical turning point that changes the course of the play. However, it is difficult to consider the actual murder onstage in V, 2 as part of the falling action. Other scholars define Desdemona's killing as the climax and Othello's realisation of his error and ensuing suicide as the falling action of the play.

Foreshadowing (or anticipation) occurs when characters unwittingly speak about the fate that awaits them. Convinced of Desdemona's loyalty, Othello answers Brabantio's warning that she might deceive him like her father with: '*My life upon her faith!*' (I, iii, l. 290) – a promise he makes good on in V, 2 when he finds her innocent. Both

Desdemona and Othello speak of their own deaths in connection with the strong feelings they experience at the instant. Othello, when he sees her after disembarking in Cyprus, says, '*If I were now to die, 'twere now to be most happy [...]*.' (II, i, ll. 182–183) to which Desdemona replies she hopes that their love and happiness will only increase. As a matter of fact, Othello would have died happily, if Iago had not begun his fiendish insinuations. Desdemona stresses her willingness to help Cassio with the promise she will '*rather die than give thy cause away*' (III, iii, ll. 27–28), which turns out to come true.

The most obvious example of anticipation is presented in IV, 3, when Desdemona's death is foreshadowed (see the following paragraph on 'atmosphere' in this section, p. 83).

The short space of time in which the tragedy happens creates more *suspense*, since physical actions follow each other quickly and emotions, such as Othello's inner turmoil, and dramatic scenes, such as the two sword-fight scenes, are shown in quick succession. In fact, the day after the couple has spent their wedding night in Cyprus is the day on which Othello kills Desdemona. While act I is shown in real time, Shakespeare makes use of *double time* in the rest of the play to hasten the unfolding of the plot. There would have been no time for the alleged affair between Cassio and Desdemona, but they are said to have made love often (IV, i, ll. 83–84), or even '*a thousand times*' (V, ii, l. 210). Emilia has been asked to steal the handkerchief '*a hundred times*' (III, iii, l. 293), although she has just begun her service the day before. Bianca says she has not seen Cassio for a week, who only disembarked the day before (III, iv, l. 167). With this device, the implausible time span is disguised and the tension of the play heightened.

More suspense is induced by the planning of the characters' deaths, the moments just before the stabbings occur, and Desdemona's smothering. As Iago shares his plots with the viewers, they will feel suspense when watching him ensnare the others and wonder how his downfall will come about.

Dramatic irony is a stylistic device used by playwrights to let the audience know more than the characters on stage. Some examples taken from IV, 2 are: Emilia draws the correct conclusion that a self-serving villain is poisoning Othello's mind, yet she isn't able to identify him. The villain she suspects is present on stage, and her railing reaches the correct addressee, Iago, who tries to stop her from speaking too loud so that nobody hears her. Desdemona asks Iago, the very man responsible for her unhappiness, what she should do and follows his advice.

Mirroring adds complexity to a plot and shows the high dramaturgical skill of the writer who can make a point on several levels. It describes a parallel action or a similar plot in a play or characters that try to achieve the same goal but have different traits which sometimes complement each other.

The intended murders are mirrored: Iago and Roderigo hatch the plot to kill Cassio, while Iago promises to kill Cassio and Othello makes plans to kill his wife. Iago's profound deception of Othello is mirrored in the seduction of Roderigo. When Iago is able to deceive so many others undetected, he becomes even more cunning. Roderigo's deceit could be seen as a comic variation of Othello's deception, which happens on a grander and more tragic scale as it leads to Desdemona's murder and Othello's suicide.

Three characters who are being deceived find out, at roughly the same time, how greatly they were tricked by Iago: first Roderigo, then both Emilia and Othello. Iago stabbing Roderigo and his wife is paralleled, too. In the final confrontation between Iago and Cassio, their earlier rivalry is mirrored, only that at this point a double reversal of fortune has taken place. Cassio lost the lieutenancy and Iago gained it, but now Iago is at Cassio's mercy.

In *Othello*, Shakespeare has included two extremely ***short scenes*** often cut out in performances, but they have an important function in the inner logic of the play's structure. In II, 2, a herald informs the Cypriots that celebrations are in order. The previous scene shows the arrival of the Venetian ships with the major characters and the subsequent scene set in the evening begins with Othello instructing the guard to maintain order. These two scenes could not follow each other directly, as the passage of time from day to night must be made clear.

The proclamation also prepares for the action of drinking and brawling that ensues.

There are merely six lines in III, 2 showing Othello on his way to inspect the fortifications in Cyprus and asking Iago to run an errand. Nevertheless, the scene has several important functions. It reminds the audience of Othello's position in Cyprus and shows him as a competent leader who lives up to his job. Apart from that, Iago as Othello's antagonist has had more stage time so far than Othello as the titular character in act II.

If the scene were cut, Cassio's encounter with Desdemona would directly follow Emilia's promise to arrange the very same meeting, when supposedly some time should have elapsed between these two events. In addition to that, as Othello orders Iago to meet him on the fortifications after Iago's errand, this allows both to re-enter together at the same instant when Cassio is talking to Desdemona. Since Iago has involved Emilia in the arrangement, he knows about the details and can perfectly time the moment of their entry.

Owing to the genre, the ***atmosphere*** in tragedies is often gloomy in character with the plot and the violent action that is to be expected. In *Othello*, many dramatic scenes are set at night or in darkness with characters not clearly visible, which adds to their irritation and perplexity and simultaneously raises suspense. The first two scenes of act I take place in the dark streets of Venice, where shouting occurs, a father assembles a search party for his daughter and then confronts the man who ran away with her. A fight between two groups of men is narrowly avoided and a mood of aggression is evoked, which creates a gripping spectacle for the audience. Before the next fierce confrontation occurs in II, 3, a moment of comic relief is shown, in which Iago sings songs and Cassio and other men are getting drunk to celebrate Othello's wedding. The scene depicts socialising, talking about who can hold more drink and what drink does to people, which amuses the spectators and forms a striking contrast to the controversy that follows. Roderigo and Cassio fight each other with swords and wound Montano, who tries to stop them. Here, a mood of danger and death is created and made worse by the audience's knowledge that it would not have happened without Iago's involvement.

In the many scenes, where Iago talks to Othello insistently to convince him of Desdemona's infidelity, they are alone on stage having intense conversations. Now and then one of them leaves to re-enter again soon, which allows the remaining character to reveal what he thinks and feels to the audience in a monologue. For the viewers, this creates the impression of being an accomplice to the crimes they are plotting and conveys an atmosphere of discomfort. In addition, compassion and worry for the victims are aroused, particularly when Iago and Othello, on their knees, swear to kill Cassio and Desdemona in an almost religious atmosphere.

In act IV, 3, the mood created is characterised by foreboding and a sense of doom. It foreshadows the tragedy one can expect after Othello's often voiced determination to kill Desdemona and his abusive treatment of her in IV, 1 and IV, 2, where he insults and strikes her. In the 'Willow scene', several elements contribute to an ominous atmosphere: Desdemona speaks about her wedding sheets she wants to be turned into shrouds if she dies before Emilia, she remembers the unhappy love story of her mother's maid Barbary and sings a sad song about death and sorrow. In the song, the metaphorical image of a willow, a symbol of sadness and death, is used.

Moreover, the function of this scene is to offer a moment of respite before the expected storm, made more painful for the audience by their expectation of what is to come. The dark side of love is mirrored with Barbary's song, which foreshadows the tragic ending of the play.

The action gathers speed in V, 1, where Cassio is wounded and Roderigo stabbed by Iago, again in a dark street where the characters can hardly see each other. The wounded men's cries and Bianca's loud wailing convey a mood of danger, death and grief. Finally, the culmination of the violent action is reached in V, 2, when Othello commits murder and suicide and Iago stabs Emilia in a cowardly move. Since the audience must experience the murder of an innocent woman and the suicide of her killer, who mourns for her when it is too late, the intended effect tragedy should have on the viewers, namely to evoke pity and fear, is achieved. Seeing three dead characters on the bed, and a culprit whose punishment is not executed on stage, will arouse a mood of gloom and devastation for the audience.

Coping with Exam Papers

The study of *Othello* in class will require you to write about the play either in coursework, for term papers or presentations, or in final examinations. In the following part, you will find guidance on writing for different tasks.

Writing about characters

When asked to write about a ***main character***, it is advisable to follow his or her journey through the play with special attention to the moments when they change and to what exactly has influenced them to do so. Instead of compiling a list of character traits, identify individual actions that define a character and think about what they are ready to do in view of achieving their aims.

Reading only the lines these characters speak from the beginning to the end of the play and writing down the action significant to their development will help to analyse the motivation of a protagonist. A good playwright never has his characters utter a wordy dialogue for its own sake but sticks to what is important to convey about the character. Each protagonist has a 'need' or 'objective' he or she wants to achieve in each scene, and it is worthwhile noting what it is. Additionally, they are hindered by an obstacle or totally blocked by an antagonist and either succeed in winning against all odds or fail. This struggle creates suspense for the audience and makes watching the characters in action interesting.

Some protagonists have an overall objective that is pursued throughout the whole play, e.g. Iago, who wants to take revenge and destroy Othello's marriage, or Roderigo, who believes he can still win Desdemona's heart with Iago's help and does everything to accomplish his goal.

The main characters are also placed within a social and political setting that might clash with their personal situation and are analysed in their respective dilemma. The title of the play *Othello, the Moor of Venice* already describes Othello as a foreigner in an all-white society. Another illustration of this conflict are the circumstances Desdemona finds herself in, who is constrained by her society's values and openly opposes them for love. Either the psychology of the character can be the centre of attention (e.g. Othello's jealousy or Desdemona's readiness to forgive) or the society they live in (e.g. women die for men's honour in a male-dominated society).

An analysis of ***minor characters*** is focused on what their function is in relation to a protagonist or the play's structure. Taking a closer look at Bianca's or Roderigo's contribution to the play will show their impact on the action. At the beginning, Roderigo is more easily manipulated by Iago than in act IV, 2, where he angrily demands his jewels back from Iago and might reveal to Desdemona what his plots are. Here Iago has to improvise and find good arguments to keep Roderigo on track. He does so by acknowledging Roderigo's frustration and promising an immediate result for the next day. Thus, Iago's skills are more appreciated, who even managed to turn Roderigo into an assassin. If Roderigo were only seen as foolish and no threat at all, Iago's masterful manipulation of him would be undervalued. In a similar way, Iago's ability to incorporate Bianca's late and surprising appearance in his schemes underlines his quick-witted nature. Not only does he estimate Cassio's reactions correctly when Iago talks to him about Bianca, but he also asks the right questions, e.g. if Cassio will marry her. This exactly produces the gestures and laughter of Cassio he wants Othello to observe.

A further example is Cassio's entreaty to make Bianca copy the strawberry pattern of the handkerchief which leads to Bianca's suspicion that he betrays her. She gives it back to him and leaves in a huff. Without these actions, Othello could not see the hard evidence of Desdemona's guilt and would not come to the ultimate conclusion that Iago's accusations are true. Besides, when the viewers see the handkerchief passing from one hand to another and note each character's different attitude to it, this endows the prop with the importance it has for the plot and it is a visible representation of the jealousy it evokes.

Comparison of characters

Another way to evaluate characters is to compare them to each other either as individuals or as figures invented for a dramatic purpose. In the section 'Language, Style and Dramatic Devices' (p. 82), a character's function as a foil or when used in mirroring is explained. Some examples are:

- Cassio and Roderigo are Italian gentlemen, but very unlike each other.
- Cassio and Iago are made Othello's lieutenant for different reasons.
- They are both wounded in the leg although their attacker's aim was to kill them.
- Brabantio as well as Othello are unable to live with the loss of Desdemona.

The respective tasks in German final exams require comparisons drawn between characters from a literary or non-fictional text and those in the play the students have studied in class. To do so, study the information the given text offers about the characters and look for suitable points of comparison. Note down what is similar and what is different to the protagonists in the play. It is very likely that the task will not deal with minor characters. Sometimes, you are also expected to give an evaluation of the character. In your text, explain your points of comparison and give reasons for choosing them. Begin writing your text by pointing out in which way the characters from the exam text resemble those of the play before you point out their dissimilarities. This way, your comparison will be more concise, you will avoid repetition and save time. You may point out, too, whether you think the resemblances are more important than the differences or vice versa.

Writing about the themes of a play

Each Shakespearean play deals with several themes which are exemplified on three different levels, i.e. on the personal level of the characters, on one that concerns the society or nation they live in, and on a supernatural or cosmic level. In *Othello*, the latter is not treated as extensively as in other plays (e.g. the appearance of witches in *Macbeth* or that of his father's ghost in *Hamlet*). Here, there are only brief references to other-worldly elements, such as Brabantio's suspicion that Othello might have used witchcraft to enchant his daughter, and Othello's tale of the handkerchief's magic qualities.

Some of the relevant themes in *Othello* are: jealousy, honour, chastity, appearance and reality, justice, religion, virtue and vice, loss, chaos and order, and hierarchy in society.

When preparing your answer, point out which characters and actions are related to the theme and find short quotations to illustrate it when you are allowed to use the book. Spend some time thinking this through, because there will be more examples than first come to mind. A typical exam question could read:

> *In every tragedy, a sense of waste is displayed. Not just lives are lost, but also other features of human life. Taking into account the characters in* **Othello**, *comment on what they lose and which effect this has on the viewers.*

Discussing topics and writing comments

These assignments often include a quote or a statement which invites discussion on a wider scope, e.g.:

> *Critics have argued that* **Othello** *is the wrong title, because it is really Iago's play.*

If you are asked to comment on an issue, you have to give your personal opinion and support or refute what the task suggests. In a discussion task, you have to look at an issue from different angles and find pros and cons.

When you have to discuss a quote, it is required that the quote is first interpreted and explained before the actual discussion begins.

You are expected to know the contents of *Othello* well, but no summary of the plot or descriptions of characters should be included. To comment or discuss a topic, choose relevant details from the play to support your point. Devise a clear line of argument with a sense of direction – your aim is to persuade the reader of your point of view. Quotes should only be included when they serve the argument, not just for decoration. When analysing events or characters, there should be references to the themes of the play, e.g. the value of trust in love, the attitudes towards jealousy shown or the importance of reputation in *Othello*.

Analysing an extract from the play or an extract from a literary or non-fictional text

Highlight what you are asked to do in the task and read the passage several times in order not to miss any important information. Many students leave out part of an assignment because they do not check the task again once they have started writing. There can be up to three different aspects that need to be dealt with in one task. Think about the context of the passage and why it has probably been chosen in the light of the study done in class during the semester so far or why an exam board might have picked it for a final examination.

Typically, there will be three sections:

1 – A *comprehension question* in the form of a brief summary or outline of the passage given

2 – An *analysis of the language* or stylistic devices (choice of words, connotations, syntax, imagery) and the effect they have on the reader

3a – An *evaluation* in the form of a comment, a comparison or a discussion of a quote or specific aspect

or   3b – A *creative writing task* referring to the play and topics raised in the extract in a prescribed text format

In a **comprehension task** you are expected to prove that you have understood the contents of the given extract. You are supposed to sum up in your own words either the whole text or just the required aspects. Do not include quotes from the text, examples or explanations and refrain from giving your personal opinion or adding information. The point is to sum up specific information, not to rephrase the whole text in its original length. While studying the text, divide it up into sections – you could find suitable headings for them in your draft as well. In your introductory sentence, refer briefly to the central idea of the passage and, if you deal with a non-fictional text, the title of the text, the text type, the author's name and the source of the text.

When asked to do an *analysis* of the text, you have to study the underlying meaning on an abstract level and point out the means the author has used to achieve a certain effect on the reader. This can concern the structure of a text, narrative techniques (e.g. point of view, mode of presentation: showing/telling, atmosphere), stylistic devices (e.g. contrast, repetition, imagery) or the choice of words (e.g. neutral/colloquial register, tone).

Instead of listing stylistic means one by one, chronologically as they appear in the text, combine elements that belong together meaningfully when you explain their effect, e.g. how a character's fear is shown in what he does and says or what others say about him. When giving evidence from the text, quote words or short phrases with the line reference only and do not copy full sentences. Here, too, no personal comment should be added.

To learn more about writing an *evaluation* of a text, read what is said above in the paragraphs 'Writing about characters', 'Writing about the themes of a play' and 'Discussing topics and writing comments'.

Creative writing tasks may appear easy at first sight, but they require the same input in regard to the knowledge of the play's content and the examination of particular aspects like an evaluation task. There are several formats:

- Writing a diary entry, a letter, an obituary etc. from the perspective of a character, often a bystander or a minor character of the play
- Devising a new scene for the play, e.g. of an offstage event or a different ending in modern English
- Writing a speech for a specific target audience to discuss a point or give a personal opinion

- Writing a letter to a newspaper editor or a person connected in some way with the topic
- Writing an article for a newspaper or magazine

General points

- Before you start on any writing task, first collect ideas and key words in a draft (do not write full sentences here). Narrow down your material to select only what is important to the point you want to make. Then rearrange your material in a way that is meaningful to you, e.g. in a mind map, a diagram, a table or a rough outline.
- Use the simple present tense when writing about the means an author has used or about characters and situations.
- Structure your text by using paragraphs and linking words. When writing a comment or discussing a topic, refer to the task in the introduction, arrange the main body clearly (in discussions, first give the arguments you do not support, then the ones you do, with the best argument coming last) and present your personal conclusion in the last part.
- Avoid repetition and superfluous fillers like 'kind of', 'somehow', 'of course' etc.
- Put quotes into inverted commas ('...') and do not merely use them as decoration, but only to underline a point or prove an argument.
- Make life easy for your examiners by numbering pages and tasks. Make changes and additions clear with asterisks or footnotes and indicated page numbers where they can find them.
- Leave sufficient time to reread your work and correct mistakes.

 # Written Test

Tasks

Read ll. 1–89 in V, 2.

CONTENT

1 Outline the situation and the conversation in this excerpt.

LANGUAGE

2 Analyse Othello and Desdemona's language (e.g. sentence structure, key words, stylistic devices, imagery) to show how Shakespeare creates character, atmosphere and theatrical effect.

DISCUSSION / COMMENT

3 Comment on the dramatic effect this scene has on the viewers and explain in which way the elements of stagecraft (e.g. conflict, timing, suspense, dramatic irony) contribute to it.

WRITING A LETTER

4 After having watched a performance of *Othello*, you are in two minds about whether a student audience should see the play. Write a letter to the director of the theatre company in which you explain your mixed feelings about the violence shown and the possibility of conveying unintended messages.

Expected answers

1

Othello enters the room while Desdemona is sleeping in their bed. Before she wakes up, he looks at her and is touched by her beauty. He finally determines that she has to die because otherwise she will betray more men. Othello is moved to tears and kisses her. When she awakes, Othello asks her to pray and to confess her sins in a serious tone. He tells her he is about to kill her. Desdemona is shocked when he accuses her of unfaithfulness. She denies having an affair with Cassio and having given the handkerchief to him, which Othello refutes by saying that he saw it in his hands. When he tells Desdemona that Cassio has admitted to sleeping with her and that he is already dead, she weeps. Othello takes this as further proof of her guilt. She pleads earnestly for her life, but he remains adamant and smothers her with a pillow.

2

When Othello watches his sleeping wife, he is depicted as calm and thoughtful. His measured verse reflects this state of mind. In ll. 1–22 Othello repeats some phrases several times, which almost gives an impression of musicality ('*it is the cause*'; '*put out the light*'; '*one more [kiss]*'). He uses imagery to compare her to marble statues, light he will extinguish or a rose he will pluck. These poetic expressions form a striking contrast to what he plans to do. An antithesis, which underlines his inner turmoil, can be found in l. 20 ('*so sweet was ne'er so fatal*') and ll. 21–22 ('*this sorrow's heavenly; it strikes where it doth love*'). After Desdemona has woken up, he gives her short orders ('*well, do it, and be brief*', l. 30; '*Peace, and be still!*', l. 46) and insults her: '*O perjured woman!*' (l. 63); '*Down, strumpet!*' (l. 80), which expresses his anger. That is also the reason why he says: '*thou dost stone my heart*' (l. 63) or '*For to deny each article with oath cannot remove nor choke the strong conception that I do groan withal.*' (ll. 54–56) and wants her to say the prayer quickly ('*solicit for it straight*', l. 28). Othello's unshakeable conviction that he does a righteous deed condoned by God lets him refer to heaven (ll. 27; 32; 63), in fact wishing heaven may have mercy on her (ll. 32; 57) and saying '*amen*' (ll. 34; 57). According to Othello, there is no contradiction in not wanting to kill her soul (l. 32) and actually murdering Desdemona. He even thinks his deed a '*sacrifice*' (l. 65) and that he is merciful when he does it quickly to spare her pain (ll. 87–89). Othello uses very short sentences that sometimes seem laconic: '*Ay, I do [talk of killing].*' (l. 33) or '*It is too late.*' (l. 84), which reveals his determination. When he is reminded of the handkerchief, Othello becomes more enraged and repeats himself ('*I saw [the] handkerchief*', ll. 62; 66) and exclaims in fury '*O perjured woman!*' (l. 63). How much his jealousy plagues him is shown in the hyperbole '*Had all his hairs been lives, my great revenge had stomach for them all.*' (ll. 75–76). Desdemona's reaction to Cassio's death provokes him even more ('*Out, strumpet! Weep'st thou for him to my face?'*, l. 78) and he expresses his cold fury in a string of short sentences (ll. 80–85) before he smothers her.

Desdemona's language forms a contrast to Othello's in that her expression is full of heartfelt emotion. When she pleads with him to let her live, she utters sounds of woe (*'O'*, ll. 74; 79; 85 and *'Alas!'*, ll. 29; 77) and uses the word *'hope'* (ll. 33; 45) to sway him. Her anxiety is reflected in the word *'fear'* that she repeats three times (ll. 35–39). Initially believing that all is well, Desdemona is soon frightened by Othello's strange behaviour when he urges her to pray. Her questions *'Alas, my lord, what do you mean by that?'* and *'Talk you of killing?'* (ll. 29; 33) disclose her worry. She hopes to stop him by referring to *'mercy'* (ll. 34; 57; 58). In her deadly terror, the references to heaven and God are simply put and spoken very naturally (*'Then heaven have mercy on me!'*, ll. 33–34; *'Then Lord have mercy one me!'*, l. 57; *'O Lord, Lord, Lord!'*, l. 86). Desdemona interprets Othello's feelings accurately when she describes his body language (*'you are fatal then when your eyes roll so'*, ll. 37–38; *'[…] why gnaw you so your nether lip? Some bloody passion shakes your very frame […].'*, ll. 43–44), and calls these signs *'portents'* (l. 45). In spite of the situation, she keeps calling Othello *'my lord'* respectfully (ll. 24; 25; 29; 69; 79). The repetition of *'never'* when affirming her innocence emphasises her fear and urge to avert her fate (ll. 58; 59; 61; 67). To illustrate her disbelief at Othello's accusations short questions are used: *'How? Unlawfully?'* (l. 70) and *'[…] what, is he dead?'* (l. 74).

Desdemona's pleas are spoken in exclamations or half sentences (e.g. *'But half an hour!'*, l. 83; *'But while I say one prayer!'*, l. 84). Her protestations of love for Othello are straightforward and simply put: *'I never did offend you in my life […].'* (ll. 58–59) and *'They [her 'sins'] are loves I bear to you.'* (l. 40).

The blank verse spoken by both Othello and Desdemona in their dialogue is irregular, which indicates that emotions are running high.

3
The dramatic effect of watching a murder on stage is huge, even if the viewers know that actors create an illusion for them. It is worsened by the fact that the spectators have seen it coming for a long time and suspense has built up gradually to this climactic moment (anticipation). The audience knows that Desdemona is blameless and must wit-

ness her undeserved death that was only brought about by Iago's intrigues and is caused by a man who once loved her deeply. This creates a feeling of senselessness and evokes pity for the victim.

The bedroom setting with only one candle for light, a sleeping woman and her husband looking at her could have conveyed a peaceful and loving mood in different circumstances. But here the contrast to what Othello is plotting to do is striking. The fact that he kisses her and is almost moved to desist from his purpose kindles the futile hope for a happy ending. However, Othello's self-righteousness and his belief that he serves justice and performs a sacred ritual ('*sacrifice*') horrifies the viewers whom he tells while crying '*cruel tears*' that he must act because he loves. Once again, a brief moment of normal marital life is depicted when Desdemona wakes up and asks him if he will come to bed before he interrogates her like an executioner about her very last prayer.

Othello's coldly uttered attempt to ensure that her soul will go to heaven marks the beginning of the couple's conflict and frightens Desdemona. Her description of his rolling eyes, bitten lip and shaking body gives the actor playing Othello's part a clue of how Shakespeare wanted this to be performed. His fearsome presence and readiness to attack opposed to her defensive posture, still lying in bed, contribute to the dramatic effect. Dramatic irony is used when Othello tells Desdemona that Cassio is dead, while the spectators are conscious of the actual outcome of the fight. Desdemona is not, and so she grieves for a pointless death she will soon share. Ironically, this fuels Othello's jealous rage even further, and the action speeds up with emotions running high, which renders the scene even more suspenseful. The following dialogue consists of pleas for mercy and their rejection, which is spoken in short sentences and quick succession. The effect achieved is that of running out of time before the catastrophe is going to happen. A climax is reached with Desdemona's begging for more time, first for a day, then half an hour and finally only the few minutes a prayer might last. Othello's merciless answer is: '*It is too late.*' (V, ii, l. 84), and the audience will feel sorrow for this injustice. Only in this scene does Othello directly name Cassio as Desdemona's alleged lover and he rejects her suggestion to have him interviewed on the case. He claims he has seen the handkerchief in Cassio's hands and that the latter has confessed to having had sex with Desdemona, which is another instance of dramatic irony since Iago merely told him so. While Emilia is shouting from outside the room to be let in, Othello notices that Desdemona is still alive, and, almost as if it were a mercy killing, continues to smother her in order to cause her no unnecessary pain. Once more, this arrogant conviction of doing what is just while committing a base crime is painful to watch, and the spectators will be emotionally upset by this experience.

4

The text should be written in the format of a letter in neutral English with the addresses of the sender and the recipient, the date, a salutation, and a complimentary close.

The first paragraph should contain a reference to the performance of the play and the explanation of what motivated the student to write to the director. The rest of the letter should show a clear structure with an introduction, a main body and a conclusion. All points should be substantiated with arguments, reasons and examples.

The following points could be made:
- general statements about the importance of Shakespeare's plays
- references to the teaching of his plays in English classes
- thoughts about the difference between adult and student audiences
- an evaluation of the performance with an explanation of the student's personal reactions
- the unnerving experience of watching the cold-blooded murder of an innocent woman
- the different impact of violence on stage and in films on viewers
- the unintended effect of enforcing racial prejudices
- suggestions how these difficulties could be overcome
  (e.g. by having more black actors in the cast, not just the one playing Othello or not showing the murder in such a way that it is painful to watch)